IN ANSWER TO THE CRY

IN ANSWER
TO THE CRY

Dorothy Yglesias

Author of
The Cry of a Bird

WILLIAM KIMBER · LONDON

First published in 1978 by
William Kimber & Co. Limited
Godolphin House, 22a Queen Anne's Gate
London SW1H 9AE

© Dorothy Yglesias, 1978
ISBN 0 7183 0046 7

This book is copyright. No part of it may be reproduced in any form without permission in writing from the publishers except by a reviewer who wishes to quote brief passages in connection with a review written for inclusion in a newspaper, magazine or radio broadcast.

MADE AND PRINTED IN GREAT BRITAIN BY
THE GARDEN CITY PRESS LIMITED
LETCHWORTH, HERTFORDSHIRE
SG6 1JS

To
Pog
and
Neverest

Contents

		Page
	Preface	13
I	In the Beginning	15
II	A New Home and Old Friends	22
III	The Birds of the Village	36
IV	A Prickly One	48
V	Charlie and Oliver	53
VI	Badgers and Seals	62
VII	Newcomers to the Hospital	74
VIII	The Dark Shadow Falls	87
IX	The *Torrey Canyon*	110
X	The Birds Play Their Part	124
XI	The Bell Still Rings	131
XII	From Far and Near	141
XIII	Our Crisis Year	152
XIV	The Lights go on	158
XV	Wise Old Owls and Strong-minded Gannets	163
XVI	Ducks and Other Patients	175
XVII	Survival	184
	Epiloque	193
	Appendix: Species of birds admitted to the hospital	198

Illustrations

PAGE 29
Dorothy Yglesias feeding an ex-patient
(David Hills)

PAGE 30
Tinker
Hospital steps and Neil's bell
Outsiders who all demand attention
(Syndication International)

PAGE 63
Pog's *Spirit of Flame*
(David Hills)
Pog's *The Man Alive*
(David Hills)
Pog working at her studio window

PAGE 64
Oiled swans from the Falmouth river
The Poggles at 'Buckingham Palace'

PAGE 65

A sick shag
(James Myers)
Guillemots inspecting their quarters
(Lauren Hutchens)
Luisa the badger
(H.G. Welby)

PAGE 66

Albert Ross
(James Myers)
Oliver, the rook
(Lauren Hutchens)
The trust of a wild bird

PAGE 99

The *Torrey Canyon* disaster
(Syndication International)

PAGE 100

Puffin, 'Tom Thumb'
A chance encounter
(Lauren Hutchens)
Oil Victim

PAGE 101

Oiled guillemot is handed in to Peggy Bell
(James Myers)
'Is there hope?'
(James Myers)

PAGE 102

Great northern diver with an injured leg
Maggie, the magpie
(Lauren Hutchens)
Baby gulls
(Lauren Hutchens)

PAGE 135

'If you can awaken a child's awareness . . .'
(Syndication International)

PAGE 136

Immature gannet
(James Myers)
Swan recovering
Olga awaiting permission from a gannet
(Amy Myers)

PAGE 137

Pam tends an injured barn owl

PAGE 138

Gannet before cleansing
Gannets after cleansing
(Amy Myers)
Gannets released to freedom

PAGE 171

Dodo waiting for a phone call
Bumble and Bee

PAGE 172

Baby tawny owl, Misty
(Harry G. Welby)

Line illustrations Page

The wharf at Mousehole harbour 19
  (Sketch by A.L. Collins from *The Land's End* by W.H. Hudson)
Jackdaws on the roof 37
  (Sketch by A.L. Collins from *The Land's End* by W.H. Hudson)
Mount's Bay and south west Cornwall 42
The hospital diary for 6th September 1975 78
The hospital diary for 25th March 1967 90
The hospital diary for 26th March 1967 91
The area of the *Torrey Canyon* disaster 112
The Scilly Islands 115
Area vulnerable to pollution from the *Torrey Canyon* 121
Letter from a visitor 189

Preface

This preface to my new book is written with true thankfulness that our Wild Birds' Hospital and Sanctuary is still surviving after the last few difficult years, beginning in 1975 when the RSPCA were forced by financial reasons to cease to maintain it. This they had done since 1960 when they generously took it over from my sister and myself who started it in 1928.

We were greatly encouraged when a local committee was quickly formed to help our sanctuary to carry on, facing the great difficulty of getting enough funds to cover immediate expenses. The children of Mousehole instantly started raising money to help the birds, and many living in the district did their utmost to come to the rescue.

This was followed by publicity given in the local and national press, and the BBC, resulting in a wonderful response from the public. But we still have a long way to go before permanent financial backing is assured.

Above all, we appreciated the determination of our loyal staff to stand by us and the sanctuary, come what may.

Now I must add my personal gratitude to the members of the staff who have made it possible for me to write this book. They are the warden, Mrs Olga Penrose, Mrs Peggy Bell and Miss Pamela Baines. First for their dedication to the work of the hospital and then for all their help and contributions for this book based on the records they have so faithfully kept over these last years, when my

In Answer to the Cry

sister and I have no longer been actively engaged in the daily routine of the hospital, as in the early days.

These experiences I have been able to incorporate into the book in a way which would not have been possible without their help.

My heartfelt thanks also for his assistance go to one of our oldest friends in Mousehole – the village that he, like my sister and myself, loves so well.

Now our final triumph is to have reached this, our Golden Jubilee Year, beginning with our first bird in 1928 and continuing up to the present to receive those birds still needing sanctuary in 1978.

Fifty years, which have passed like a dream, yet still live in memories of those days we shall never forget.

DOROTHY YGLESIAS
Mousehole, Cornwall

I
In the Beginning

When one looks back over more than eighty years of life, a happy childhood seems the greatest blessing that can be given one. My memories tell me it was so with our family. Our father was an artist, gifted and sensitive, with true values as to what mattered in life. Love and loyalty stood high; money came last.

When first married, he and our mother, who was also an artist, lived in London in Fitzroy Street; but when their first-born, my brother, was on the way, it was decided the important thing was to find a real home as the right background for the child. This was found in that loveliest part of London, St John's Wood. The house was in Grove End Road, with the gardens opposite at a lower level, making the outlook from our windows just a heavenly expanse of sky, with glorious sunsets.

I was born two years after my brother, Laurie; then came our sisters, Phyllis and Mary. Phyllis from her childhood was known as Pog and was so called till the end of time.

Our home, with its large rambling garden, a big studio detached from the house, with two tubs of blue agapanthus lilies standing on either side of the entrance, is the memory that stays with me always.

The studio was a kind of 'holy of holies' to us three children (Laurie was then at boarding-school). We were allowed in there every Sunday afternoon. Our father sat on the couch with a large home-made scrapbook in his hands and we grouped ourselves around him. The pictures in the book were mostly taken from the Bible or from illustrated anecdotes about animals. Each of us in turn chose the story we wanted to hear, and our father would switch his imagination from a stray dog to the Miracle of the Loaves and Fishes in such a way as to make it all come to life.

We dearly loved the miracles and thought they brought a new and splendid dimension into this earthly life. They solved so many problems, as we were to find out in the years that followed.

What happy times they were. The garden was our playground where we invented every kind of game from Ghosts to Cops and Robbers. An artist friend of our father's who had forgotten the number of our house, asked a policeman if he knew where the artist Mr Yglesias lived? The man replied, 'Oh, you mean the artist with the noisy family? He lives at number 14'. The friend was amused, but Mother was *not!*

The artists seemed to live mostly on our side of the road and the 'gentry' on the other, which was shared by writers and actors.

Someone who added greatly to our fun was our dear Jenny, who came daily to help Mother with the cooking and housework. Her great sense of humour appealed irresistibly to us. She formed a friendship with a cook from the 'gentry' side, not far from us. They first met when taking the dogs from their respective households for a walk. Jenny had Nell our Welsh terrier bitch, an obvious mongrel with a long tail, and the cook Lord Robert Cecil's thorough-bred Chow. Jenny enquired, 'What is your dog called?' 'Togo, after Admiral Togo,' replied the cook, 'and what is yours called?' Quick as a flash Jenny answered, *'Ours* is Nell after Lord Nelson?' I can see the twinkle in her eye as she told us about it.

Childhood was followed by the adventure of growing up, still in the lovely background of our dearly loved home, with holidays spent in Sussex or Kent where my father found hidden corners of beauty for his sketches.

Life changed when he died in 1911. The year after that we came to Cornwall for a holiday for the first time, during Mary's schooldays, when Pog was an art student, and I, having left school, was ready for any adventure that might turn up.

In the Beginning

Mousehole, a fishing village near the extreme western tip of Cornwall, was where we stayed. The more we saw of it, the more we loved it and its kind and hospitable people. The rounded hills under which it nestled, the curving line of the old harbour wall which sheltered it from the power of the sea, made it the most beautiful place in the world. Here indeed was another 'home' where we renewed the happiness of our younger days. We greatly missed our father and thought how he too would have appreciated this wealth of beauty.

We came every year for our holidays, but in the second year we camped out on a farm at the top of one of the hills. The first Sunday after we arrived a trail of our village friends came up to see us, each bringing gifts of fruit, vegetables, cakes or fish. They thought we must have lost all our money to be living in a tent, something they only connected with the wandering gypsies! The lovely warmth of this sign of friendship almost reduced us to tears.

Another old inhabitant came up to Mother one evening when we were down on the quay watching the pilchard boats go to sea. He stood very close to her, put a crumpled envelope into her hand and said, 'Mrs Gleeshus, I've got £100 saved up and thought it might be a help to you. Please take it!' Love and loyalty, how right our father was, except that now 'money' had come right up to the top too, but in the right perspective. Mother expressed her deep gratitude and said she would never forget his thought for us all, and promised to tell him if ever need arose but at present we could manage on her small income.

We had always loved the hill on the southern side of the village. It was our favourite evening walk, but little did we think then that this hill was where we should eventually live and end our days. However, we gave Mother no peace until she promised to try and sell our old home in London and make a new one here.

Through one of the friendships we had formed in the village and much to our excitement Mother was eventually able to buy a long bit of meadow land actually on the hill we all loved so much, where

In Answer to the Cry

Mount's Bay spread out below us radiant in the summer with the blue seas dancing in the sunlight, in winter with great crested waves sweeping in from the ocean speaking of the eternal life of nature, the hazards and the triumphs.

The land had once been a cherry orchard and still there were old trees in the hedges covered in delicate blossom each spring; so when our new home was built we called it Cherry Orchard.

This happened in 1925 after the dear old home was sold. The foundations of Cherry Orchard were built, not only of rock and cement, but on the friendship of the one who helped us to get the land, a friendship shared with his family, which has lasted till this day.

While the house was being built we lived in a cottage nearby and Pog, through a fisherman friend, was allowed to use a net loft down on the wharf in which to develop her great love of wood, the medium in which she expressed her imaginative vision. The wood sculpture which eventually emerged as the result of those early days was reminiscent more perhaps of Epstein than of anything else that had been attempted before, its main theme being the human face and form, whether singly or in groups, reflecting in different ways the spiritual quality in our human thought.

Pog was very friendly with the boys of the village and one day a youngster came with a poor little baby jackdaw, a sorry sight, as the boy had cut its wings to prevent it flying away, and evidently had not known how to feed the bird. My sister was horrified but realised it was not cruelty but a desire to have something of his own to love and care for that had made the boy pick up the bird when he saw it fluttering on the ground, and take it home. She explained that, for the bird's sake, it would be better to leave it with her for the time. The child gladly handed it over but the poor little thing died in spite of all her efforts to save it. Help had come too late. Perhaps the seed sown unconsciously in our minds, as a result of this sad little episode, eventually grew and blossomed into what was later to become our Wild Birds' Hospital.

The windows of Pog's wharf studio looked out immediately on to the harbour, a man-made place like others of its kind around our shores that seem to complete the shape and beauty of their natural surroundings. She could see it in all its moods, most attractive perhaps at the weekend high tides when all the boats were at their moorings (there was no Sunday fishing in those days), stretching across in three long arcs from pier to pier and almost filling the harbour except for a necessary passageway through them here and there; a peaceful anchorage, where the risen water seemed to have as little movement in it as the land. The old wooden crane, that swung the baulks up or down at the harbour mouth, was still there, giving an extra significance to the scene.

Its appearance was no less interesting and typical when the tide was out. There would always be a number of fishermen down there, occupied in different ways with their own boats. One man would be stretched out on his back under a dark hull, giving it a fresh coating of tar. Here and there a boat's ladder would be slopping up against its bulwarks, with other men on deck, mending a net or a sail, splicing a rope, or attending to one or other of the numerous tasks required to keep a boat in condition and ready for sea. Perhaps a village carpenter would be at work, with hammer and plane and saw, making some change or addition to a boat or repairing a weakness discovered somewhere in its woodwork.

Often the harbour walls were covered on the inside by freshly 'barked'* nets hanging down to dry, and scores of new ropes nearly a hundred yards long were stretched tightly across above the boats from one part of the railing to another, with a fisherman at one end pulling them tighter still from time to time. But the busiest and most exciting scenes were when the boats were casting off one after the other and putting out to sea in the evenings; and then the unloading of their catches, hundreds of thousands of pilchards often, the next morning. The livelihood and all the skill and experience of the village were concentrated there.

Things are different now. The fishing boats have gone; just a few punts are left, and a score or so of new pleasure boats for use in the summer months only. The massive old mooring chains, no longer needed, are rusting away and completely buried, in places, under the coarse gravel sand. This change however has had one interesting result. There is now a wider and freer range for the wading birds that have come in increasing numbers from elsewhere, and they are more easily watched and approached across

*A fishing term meaning cleaned and cured.

In the Beginning

the bare harbour strand. The old-established village residents, chiefly the gulls and jackdaws, are still there, bathing at low tide in the stream that runs down through the centre of the harbour or preening themselves by its side. The turnstones, always the most common of the waders, leave us only at breeding time. But during the winter months other waders come and feed along the edge of the changing tide; redshanks and ringed plovers; several species of sand-pipers; knots and dunlins and others. Even in rough weather and at high tide there is always a chance of seeing something unusual; a much rarer bird perhaps, that is in poor condition and has come in to shelter from the storm. The kingfisher too may be busy then, perching on the rungs of the chain ladders and diving into the shoals of little fish that have sought refuge from the more troubled waters outside.

Pog's work was made more pleasant, if not perhaps a little helped or inspired, by such surroundings, and there are plenty of similarly placed studios now, occupied by artists of different kinds, in the fishing villages along the Cornish coastline.

II
A New Home and Old Friends

When we were settled into Cherry Orchard, Pog decided to move up from the village to a wooden hut built on the far end of our land which she then used as her studio. It was at that time, in 1928, that our involuntary hospital really began. A jackdaw found in a drainpipe with a broken wing was brought to us one day and Pog at once made the end of her hut into his house and took him in and looked after him.

As the word got round he was soon followed by another and after that it seemed that when anyone found a casualty it was brought to us. More and more birds arrived.

Pog began to get commissions for her work, and as time went on and our patients increased life began to get rather difficult. Finally Mother decided to build her a lovely studio in the garden, so she migrated, leaving the hut for the injured birds.

Her time was now spent first in making more houses and new aviaries for the birds in the old hut and then fixing a bird tray for the wild birds outside her studio window. This was necessary for her to feel 'at home' in her new quarters. It was a lovely building, with the wooden beams and the roof forming the ceiling and giving the feeling of height and space. The three big windows letting in the sun and light made it a perfect setting for her carving.

She put her bed under the 'bird window', as she called it, so that she could keep in close contact with her flying companions who

A New Home and Old Friends

soon found her out. Later some even came inside to roost on the beams on very stormy nights.

The studio was built on the highest part of our land which gave Pog a breathtaking view over the bay with the age-old St Michael's Mount standing as a sentinel on the left and the distant point of the Lizard on the right, far away out at sea, guarding the approaches to our lovely Mount's Bay. As Pog's old friend Laura Knight, the painter, once said, 'It gives you something that stays with you all your life.'

But the sound of the fishing boats putting to sea below still kept her in touch with her old studio on the wharf where she had spent those first years in Mousehole.

We were now desperately busy earning the money to care for our ever-increasing patients, Pog by her wood carving, I by growing flowers for the market in our meadows. Eventually we had to build even more home-made runs with packing-case houses for the injured herring gulls and other sea birds that were brought to us. Pog with her ingenious imagination made each house to suit every individual type of bird and they always felt at home at once.

To save the arduous task of carrying all the water needed in pails up from the house, she made a grand contrivance of hosepipes and gutters to fill various water butts and tin baths she had collected, from heaven knows where, and then connected them to the tap from the water tank at Cherry Orchard. This all worked splendidly and saved an enormous amount of time and labour. We used a great deal of water as Pog was very insistent that the rock pools she had made for the gulls must be large and deep.

The position of the hospital high above the village on the side of our steep hill, with no shelter from the south-easterly gales that sometimes swept in from the sea, did not help our attempts to build the runs. The bad weather increased the need for them as birds were brought in sick or injured by the fierce attacks of nature. We spent a lot of time struggling with the wire netting flapping in the wind as we strove to get the posts firmly in the ground, and the urgency added a spur to our efforts. But all got finished in the end with shelters facing the sun ready to receive all needing attention, rest and security.

One great benefit came from this lofty hillside setting and that was the perfect 'take-off' it provided for the large sea birds when they were fit for release. With injuries cured and plumage perfect the first real sign that a bird was ready to go was the look in its eyes which would noticeably change. Instead of concentrating on their pans and food and pools filling with running water, the day would come when they would cease to be interested in these objects but would focus their eyes on the distant horizon; the sparkling sea of freedom stretched out below the hillside on which they stood. The wire netting no longer seemed a barrier and when the door was opened they knew exactly what to do. They stretched to their full height, spread their wings — and off, into the beauty of life restored.

The number of birds needing help grew every year and we felt our Mousehole Wild Birds' Hospital and Sanctuary was firmly established just as we ourselves over the years had so firmly established our roots in Cornwall. Our aim was always to release a bird back to freedom as soon as it was ready for it; to give sanctuary to those whose injuries prevented their return to the wild but who were still capable of enjoying life in the sanctuary, and only to destroy those beyond all help and for whom a merciful death was the only answer.

The problem was that the longer we went on the greater the rising costs, and the more casualties that came the less time we had to earn the money to help them. Food of course had to be the first consideration. Fish was always expensive and essential for the diving sea birds. It had to be fresh or they did not fancy it. The ordinary herring gulls were more accommodating and we mixed their diet with brown bread soaked in the cheapest dripping we could find. Rooks, crows and jackdaws were easier; we gave them a deep pan of fresh earth and huge tussocks of grass so that they could

A New Home and Old Friends

explore for natural food of worms or insects for themselves. They loved cheese, peanuts, bits of meat, and brown bread spread with margarine and to ensure proper nourishment we would sometimes give an egg custard and wholemeal biscuits. But it all cost money, especially the packets of bird seed and insectivorous food for the little birds, mixed corn for the pigeons, and meat and rabbits for the birds of prey. However, people who brought injured birds to us were always so thankful to find this refuge that they seldom left without a contribution.

In 1945 at the end of the war and after we had been working with the birds in Mousehole for seventeen years the Royal Society for the Prevention of Cruelty to Animals (RSPCA) came to our rescue by giving financial aid with £2 a week. They also spent a great deal more money on repairing the old runs and making badly needed new ones. All this was a tremendous help.

It was at this time that we had to leave our much loved Cherry Orchard where we had been so happy for so long. Our mother had died some time before and we knew we could no longer afford to live there. So we sold the house and moved into a small bungalow, Green Hedges, which was just below the studio, both situated on the land adjoining the hospital.

This was a wonderful little haven of peace in a secluded part of our garden, the only access to the road being a long path leading to the steep hill going down in to the village. From the big window we had the same expansive outlook over the bay as Pog had from the studio. Many a time my problems found a solution by just standing there quietly gazing at its beauty.

Time went by and we got ever busier, with birds being sent to us from further and further away as the hospital became more widely known. After some years we began to realise that we were getting older and that we must try to make provision for the future. So in the late fifties, after much discussion, we decided to approach the RSPCA hoping that they might feel able to provide the solution.

In Answer to the Cry

The big step was taken and they generously agreed to take over all responsibility from us.

After this the building of a concrete main building with an office and new bird runs, a pigeon loft and also one for the owls was all put in hand. Then of course we had to train the staff who were now to be employed; a warden and her four assistants. By 1960 all was completed and we handed over our work of thirty years. We felt a little sad but were sustained by the belief that the sanctuary was to be maintained on a permanent basis and that all would be well.

Two years later I wrote a book, *The Cry of a Bird*, telling the full story of our life's work and ended on a note of thankfulness that the future was assured and of our gratitude to those who were to follow us in caring for the birds,

But those early years had been very strenuous ones. From 1928 up to the last entry in our records in 1959 we had taken in 4,066 sick or injured birds. Our first oiled bird was in 1934 and every year afterwards they had continued to come, the most tragic of our casualties, but little did we realise the devastating effects that this oil at sea was suddenly to have at a future date.

However happy we were to have the main load lifted from our shoulders, life was still full and busy. The birds saw to that. Having once admitted us to their trust and friendship they still came to our balcony at Green Hedges and to Pog's studio window, for food and shelter, both the old ones we had known and the new patients at the hospital who soon learned, when released, that we still 'belonged' as they say in Cornwall.

This link was kept intensely alive by one unforgettable jackdaw who was brought to us as a baby in 1953, having fallen down a chimney from his nest. He came the day that Mount Everest was climbed so he was given the name of Neverest! We reared him, first in my bedroom at Green Hedges, and then he was taken to the studio to learn to fly properly before release. We set him free a few

A New Home and Old Friends

weeks later from the studio window; but he constantly returned, full of excitement. When he was two years old and had chosen a wild mate he even persuaded her to come inside for short visits.

He was in his ninth year, in 1961, when we had ceased to be actively working at the hospital. This made no difference however to Neverest. He and his mate Buttons continued to look upon Pog as their slave, and they flew daily in and out of the studio, usually returning there to sleep at night.

In April 1964 they built a nest on the beams but no eggs resulted. In the following January a call of distress from Neverest early in the morning made Pog leap out of bed to find dear little Buttons lying dead. She was now about nine years old, faithful to Neverest all her life. We buried her in the rosebed under the studio window.

Soon after this Neverest returned one day with a severely damaged wing. How he managed to reach 'his sanctuary' we could not imagine; but he was right in knowing it was his only hope, as from that day he could never fly in the wild again. After treatment he was able to flutter all over the studio and slept every night on his special beam in a dark corner. His days were filled with cheerful conversation, both with Pog and the wild birds who came to the bird tray outside the window. It seemed as if he rather enjoyed flaunting his superior diet to the outsiders, almost chuckling with glee.

By 1972 he became less active, with his eyesight failing; so Pog made him a special house where he could come to no harm. In March 1973 he was very quiet, would only drink water and slept most of the time. One afternoon we were both standing by him, he in a deep sleep, when he opened his eyes widely, seemed to look directly at us, or, who knows, at something beyond, and our Neverest had gone. He had been Pog's constant companion all those years, and to this day still seems very near and will always be part of the studio. He was just twenty years old. We laid him beside Buttons, among the roses.

In Answer to the Cry

The publication of *The Cry of a Bird* brought us hundreds of letters from all parts of the world. Of one of those who wrote we have most happy memories, a young girl from America then aged thirteen years. She had read the book and wrote to the warden of the sanctuary saying she did not know if Pog and I were still there, but she had much enjoyed reading it as she too loved all nature and wild creatures. She added, 'I cannot donate money but I can donate something that will be more of *me*, my poem:

> The Cry of a Bird
> Coming from the Sea
> Where all life began
> You see a shape — the wings
> Outspread in the
> Rejoice of
> Freedom.
> It cries Farewell
> And meets the horizon.
> In harmony
> A Bird
> A live Bird

1st October 1969, USA

'Dedicated to the Wild Birds' Hospital and Sanctuary, Mousehole.

'In memory of Dorothy and Pog Yglesias, all the Birds that died in their hands and those who lived to fly and cherish life again.

Love
Megan Boyd'

I feed an ex-patient who returns daily for a snack.

Tinker, pathetic on arrival, but always happy and cheerful.

Hospital steps with Neil's bell at top.

Outsiders who all demand attention.

A New Home and Old Friends

Pog and I felt very happy to have such a lovely little epitaph. Perhaps the girls working at the hospital will put it up there when our time comes.

Other letters came from USA, Africa, Barbados, Malta, Canada, New Zealand, France, Rhodesia, Kenya, Natal, California, Guatemala, Central America, Italy, Switzerland, India, Hong Kong, Capri, Australia and Mexico.

The American letters came as a result of the USA edition. We thus made many new friends, some of whom still keep in contact with us and come to see us and the sanctuary when visiting England.

One of the Australian letters was specially valued by us. The writer said he had been in complete despair; such unbelievable cruelty was being shown to kangaroos in his country that he had been left thinking that there could be no hope for the human race. Then, by chance, he read our book; from all those thousands of miles away the message came, love and compassion still existed in an active form and his faith in humanity was revived.

When wondering if I *could* write a sequel to my first book as my publisher kindly wanted me to do, I got out my file of all these letters. As I turned the pages my heart warmed at all the encouraging words that had been written. It was late at night when I came on a letter from a Mr Heinehamp of New Zealand which ended, 'My wife and I would love to read another book on similar lines as *The Cry of a Bird* as we feel sure your pen holds many more stories.' I thought this was a kind of 'sign', so I decided to see what I could do.

The very next morning another strange thing happened. A knock on the door; a tall man on the doorstep with his wife and little boy. He introduced himself as John Harper who as a boy visitor to Mousehole in 1943 had brought to us a young herring gull in bad condition owing to a serious wound on its head. We had told him we did not hold out much hope. John had thought otherwise and had said, 'The bird must be called Dauntless.' How right he was. The bird made a complete recovery, and when later released came back daily and fed from our hands, finally returning with a mate. Both birds continued to come back to the sanctuary for twelve years.

It was a very happy meeting and John told me he still has my postcard written all those years ago saying how Dauntless was improving. His love for birds is very strong and now, as a schoolmaster, his influence on the children must be great, helping them to become aware of the need to help all suffering.

Another child's voice from past years came on our reading of a national newspaper competition, organised for young people, in which the winning essay had been written by fifteen-year-old Kenneth Mitchell.

As a small boy he had lived in Mousehole for a few years and was an ardent supporter of our Birds' Hospital. We had lost touch with him since his parents left the district. How pleased we were when we found he had chosen as the subject of his essay our Mousehole Bird Sanctuary. I feel it endows us with a quite undeserved halo which makes me hesitate to quote it. But the happiness it gave Pog and me to read quite outshines any halo. So here it is:

THE PERSON I MOST ADMIRE

I am a Cornish boy, and every day of my early life was spent near the cliffs and coast. The taste of salt on my lips as I walked in the winds. The cries of badgers in the summer evenings, flowers everywhere, free for me to pick.

In such a place as this lives a lady whom I admire most in the world, one who has given her life to the little bird sanctuary at Mousehole, the picturesque fishing village near Penzance, where the waves lash against the harbour wall and even the gulls seem to scream for mercy.

There are many kinds of waves in the world – of the air, and of the sea, but when you are Cornish and have the faculty for longing, you will search for those that take you away from the

A New Home and Old Friends

land you love so well but cannot stay in, and although I am now living far away from my native home, I can see her now, risking her life for the creatures she loved so well – climbing the high and slippery rock to answer the call of a sea bird in distress; patiently hour by hour cleaning the oil from his poor maimed body, because our beautiful sea was sometimes treacherous to all little living creatures, and modernisation, blind to beauty could make his every day a perilous existence.

Cormorants, terns, pigeons with broken wings – shot by the pellets of an airgun by thoughtless village boys in pursuit of pleasure – are welcomed with open arms by my heroine of the sanctuary.

I cannot even remember her name. I only know that when I was a very little boy and it was Sunday afternoon. Sunday! That dreaded day when I always had to sit still whilst someone had their afternoon nap – and it always seemed to be pouring with grey monotonous rain. Then I would sit by the window for hours, watching her house, hoping to see someone knock at her door with perhaps another sad little victim in his arms.

Then I would creep out and beg to be allowed to watch, maybe even to help!! Kindness, patience, humanity. These are the lessons that she unconsciously taught me. I shall remember her all my life – even through the 'Blur and Blot' of years to come.

Although our active work at the sanctuary was over, we still kept and continue to keep in constant touch, and often visited our old friends Rider and Hedger, the herring gulls that came to us in 1943. Both were casualties, each with a wing severed at the shoulder which an airman later visiting the hospital told us was probably caused, much to the man's regret, by the bird flying against the wire of the practice target towed behind a plane. The full account of their life with us is in *The Cry of a Bird*, but the end must now be told.

In Answer to the Cry

After this long life of complete contentment and devotion to each other in their own special run, we noticed one day Rider was not as active as usual, soon just lying quietly on his bed of straw all the time, until one night he just passed away in his sleep. This was in 1971 when he was twenty-eight years old. Hedger did not seem to grieve but would never accept anyone in his place. She died two years later aged thirty, and so that link with our past was also ended.

Thinking back over these bygone times has brought vividly to my mind one day, many years ago, when I was working in one of the runs and saw a complete stranger wandering around, finally stopping for a long time gazing at Rider and Hedger. I wondered 'critical or approving?' and thought I had better go and speak to him. Before I got there he came up to me with a pleased expression on his face and said, 'Thank you! This is a *real* sanctuary', in complete understanding of our attitude to the value of life, a tribute to the sense of peace and contentment given out by Rider and Hedger during their long life spent in their sanctuary home.

Another old inmate is Jimmy the Crow, brought in 1954 as a two-year-old, having originally been found when only a few days old in a deserted nest with another baby dead beside him. The two small boys who rescued him reared him up and the three of them, boys and bird, lived so closely together that Jimmy became the boss and was utterly tame. When he became beyond control he was brought to us. Still completely without fear of humans, he adopted us and nothing would alter his attitude to life. His exuberant nature and absolute trust in all mankind made it impossible to return him to the wild. It was an intensely difficult decision to make, as our aim is always to give freedom when the bird is ready for it. But we knew it was the right one for Jimmy. He is still to this day as self-possessed and interested in everything as ever. When I go up to the hospital he greets me with a Wop! wop! wop! and on having his bit of sausage or other tit-bit from me he expresses his pleasure by a long O-ooooo ouh! He has brought

A New Home and Old Friends

happiness into many lives, especially to the boy who had rescued him. He came again ten years later in 1964, as a young man, to ask what had happened to Jimmy and was delighted to be greeted by the bird whose life he had saved. Then much later on he became terribly worried about his Jimmy when he heard news of the proposed closure of the hospital. He came down to Cornwall and said he would make some arrangements as the bird must *not* be destroyed. How thankful he was when told that the sanctuary was going to carry on at all costs. Jimmy was safe. He is now twenty-five years old.

III
The Birds of the Village

The houses that cluster so closely around Mousehole harbour have changed little in the fifty years since the hospital began. Looking down from the steep hillside at the back of the village only the roof-tops can be seen, all so close together that hardly a single street or passage-way can be caught sight of anywhere between them. Their grey slates are white in places with gull droppings and are getting more and more covered with the brightly golden-coloured lichens that flourish in the damp sea atmosphere. These roofs, seeming to have no plan and huddled together at all angles, are the homes of the village gulls and jackdaws, the former building their nests occasionally behind a convenient chimney-stack and the latter down in those flues which their acute sense of smell tells them have been long disused. During the summer many baby jackdaws are brought into the hospital, some covered with soot through having fallen down these chimneys, and one of our first and most loved birds, Ben, was brought in to us after being cared for for some years by a fisherman down whose chimney he had fallen as a fledgling. He became so bossy as time went on that Pog and I regarded him as the self-appointed superintendent of the hospital! Before electricity came to the village the jackdaws maintained an active and discriminating interest too in the flues that were in constant use, and at weekends when the Sunday dinner was being cooked there was often quite a struggle amongst them to savour the smells coming up through the chimney-pot above.

The Birds of the Village

The jackdaws on our roofs are as much a part of the peaceful village atmosphere as the thin columns of smoke rising into the still air. On windy days they always gather on the lee side of a roof, just under the top ridge-tiles, with their heads only looking over, facing into the direction of the wind like wise old weather-vanes. They are lovable birds, accepting our food and hospitality but keeping to their wild state. The era of tame jackdaws I hope is over now when young boys, imitating their lively little calls, went looking for those woodlice, the 'grammar sows', that seemed to be

their favourite food and were the same dull grey colour as the birds.

Our other prolific bird – the gull – has a very special place in the minds of fisherfolk everywhere, not merely because it is a scavenger and helps to keep a harbour clean; it has its own expert knowledge of the sea and the excitement it shows out on the fishing grounds is often an indication of where the wandering shoals of pilchards and other fish are to be found. In former days, when catches were being counted and unloaded in the harbour here, they would be screaming and circling in their hundreds over the heads of busy fishermen, swooping down upon the crushed or broken fish that were being slung overboard here and there. In Mousehole such scenes have gone, but you can still see little flocks of them following in the wake of the Newlyn fishing boats as they pass quite close to us along the shore towards the fishmarket there.

The Mousehole gulls are chiefly herring gulls, but you can always see a few of the greater black backs among them and less often the smaller blackheaded variety. Although the gull is always as close to us as the jackdaw, the relationship between it and man has always been more reserved. They wait for the fish to come, and feed frantically on them when they are offered, and having had their fill are content to wait for the next time. They feed more casually then and only occasionally on the marine life of the shore, but mostly it seems not bothering to seek for food at all, content to fight for a share in the bread and other tit-bits thrown down into the harbour by the villagers, in a brief but clamorous rivalry filling the harbour with their cries. Often as one sits upon the shore a herring gull will be standing with its webbed feet on a rock only a few yards away. As you watch in silence, it knows you are there, but its cold inscrutable eyes are looking out to sea, as silent as the wide horizon line of the Atlantic beyond. 'Keep your distance from me', it seems to say; 'live and let live; and we shall get on well together as we have always done in the past.'

Of recent years there has been one change in their habits. The old horse-drawn plough that moved so slowly and turned perhaps

The Birds of the Village

only a single furrow was followed by a gull or two, even when quite a distance inland. But nowadays the faster moving tractor that opens several furrows at a time, often has a hundred gulls behind it, a harbour-full of them it almost seems, crying and snapping up a host of worms and insects of all kinds before they have time to conceal themselves beneath the surface again. The wary oyster-catcher, a familiar sight around our shores, handsome with its black and white plumage and its long orange-red bill, is also I believe seen much more frequently now feeding in the fields, often in company with turnstones when periods of stormy weather prevent them from feeding freely on the shore.

Shags are also a permanent part of our surroundings, but of the shore rather than the village, which they never enter, though sometimes you may see one or two fishing in the harbour at high tide. 'Train-i-goats' they used to be called locally, and somehow the name seems to suit them as the head and neck move like a periscope along the surface of the water. After the sudden dive for a fish below, one watches to see exactly where the shag will surface again ten or twenty yards away. It has its own Shag Rock out by St Clement's Island just offshore from Mousehole where you can often see it, and on the little rocky island itself drying its outspread wings in the sun, its dark outline in striking contrast with the smaller white forms of the gulls there. There was a time when a misguided government authority offered a shilling (5p) each for every head of shag that was brought to them, but that attitude is now happily a thing of the past.

Among the shags and gulls on the island there will always be a few curlews, their sober plumage invisible against the dark background of the rock but their unmistakable calls can be heard from the shore. Sometimes at night, when all other birds are at rest, you will hear them passing over the village with that quick 'curlie, curlie, curlie' cry, above the sound of the stream cascading into the harbour.

There are as many house sparrows in Mousehole as gulls and

jackdaws but with their drab colouring they seem mostly to be lost in their surroundings, except perhaps when you see them nibbling rather ineffectively at a crust of bread they have discovered somewhere on the ground. They rarely go down into the harbour where the rock pipit, a much more graceful creature of roughly their colour and size and known always as the shore lark by the fishermen, moves along the seaweed and other debris thrown up by the tide, or its little 'cheep' reveals its presence somewhere near. The pied wagtail will be there too uttering its 'tizzik' call and more rarely the grey wagtail, mistaken perhaps for the pied with its brisk walk and swifter little run as it picks off the insects from the damp strand, till its sudden swinging flight reveals the pure lemon-yellow of its underparts. Throughout the winter months you can occasionally see the black redstart there too.

Our commonest and most beloved land birds are often absent from a fishing village, the robins and the wrens, blackbirds and thrushes, tits and finches and other kinds, but they are nevertheless all around us here, along the more sloping parts of the coastline, by the houses at the back of the village that have little gardens of their own, and in the small 'meadows' on the higher slopes where violets and anemones and other winter and spring flowers are grown on a commercial scale. The hospital has a 'Small Birds' house especially for these garden birds. A missel thrush will be nesting up there in the fork of a tree and you will sometimes hear a raven croak as its passes overhead. Each year one listens for the return of the brave little chiffchaff, its oft repeated 'chiff-chaff' call coming from somewhere in the wooded hillside that is hidden like the bird itself in the fresh and abundant foliage of the spring. The rookery in the elm tree wood almost overhanging the village school is gone, for the trees became unsafe, a danger to the children in the playground below, and they have all been felled or lopped to half their height. The rooks' busy and excited calls at nesting times used to be a part of the village atmosphere, and over the years rooks from all around have been frequent patients at the hospital.

Our village of Mousehole is three miles west of the market town of Penzance. Both Penzance and the now major fishing port of Newlyn, closer still to us, are hidden by the Penlee headland only a few hundred yards away. The Penlee lifeboat-house is there and the disused quarry area that is the favoured resort of owls. Many owls too have been tended by us, including sometimes the little owl, a comparative newcomer to our shores. At the very head of the bay another three miles beyond Penzance is the level stretch of the Marazion marshes, the well-known haunt of waders and the many ornithologists who watch them there. It is also a favourite roosting area for starlings. Dense clouds of them can be seen converging on it from all directions in the evenings, always a wonderful sight as they wheel and turn in unison like a huge fan.

To some people the starling, with what they feel to be his rather pushing ways, is less attractive than other garden birds. But we have cared for many of them, delighting in their intelligence and bright and active personalities; each one is an individual as with all other birds.

Just a little further eastwards, where the opposite coastline of the long Lizard peninsula begins, St Michael's Mount rises; a massive outlier of granite, connected only by a narrow causeway at low tide to the mainland and surmounted by its beautiful fairy-tale castle, with the centuries-old changes of fortune that most castles seem to have and its historic link with Mont St Michel in Brittany. Described by someone once as a piece of Lyonesse lying at anchor off the shore, it is a dramatic and romantic sight from here five miles away across the inner reaches of the bay.

From St Michael's Mount southwards along that eastern side we can look across and see the different headlands and some of the long sand beaches and fishing villages there, with the Godolphin and Tregonning hills undulating inland behind them. The largest of

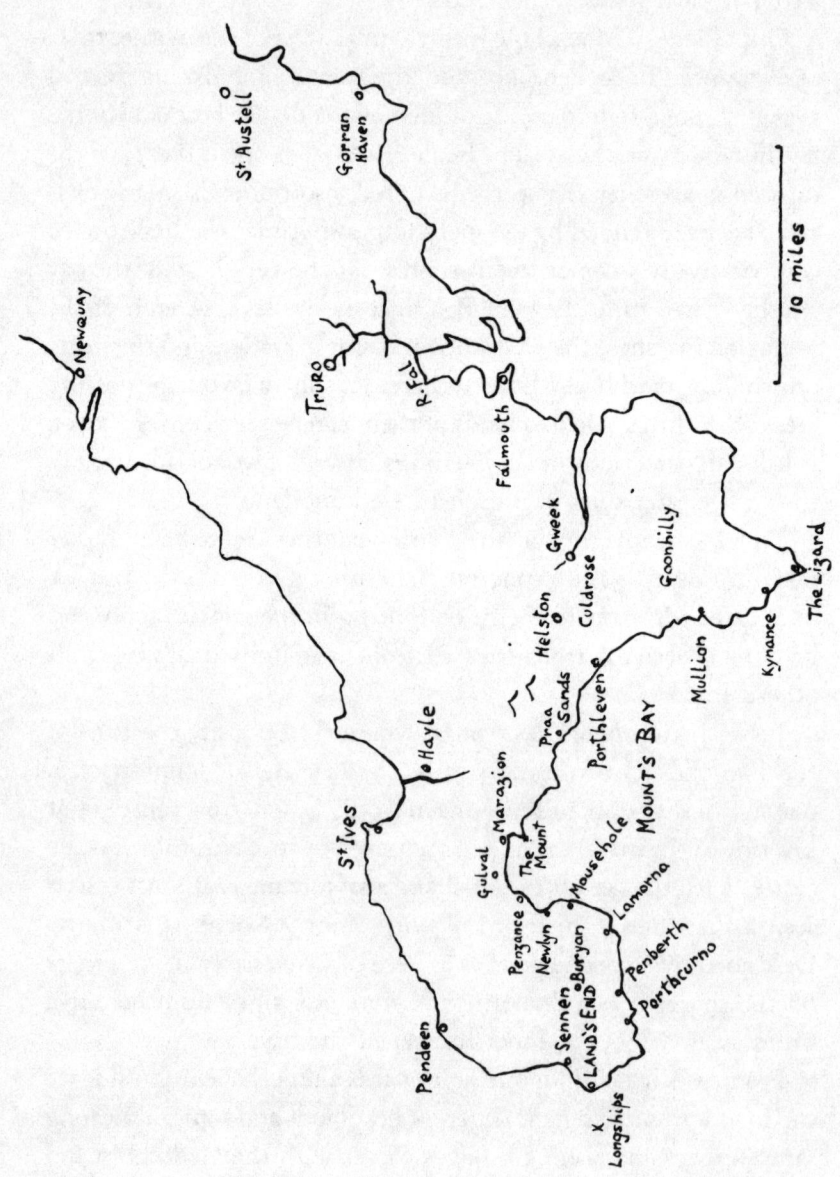

the villages is Porthleven, an old and friendly rival of Mousehole, with ten sea miles between us, but as in Mousehole itself its fishing has declined, the harbour is silting up and the Porthleven lifeboat with its proud history behind it, has gone.

Still further to the south, behind the steep drop into Mullion cove and harbour, are the now famous 'dish aerials' of Goonhilly Downs connecting us with the satellite network of the world and built on the very spot where Marconi first established wireless communication with America. Finally, past the fine coastal stretch of Kynance, is the Lizard headland with its serpentine rock and its lighthouse, the most southerly point of Britain, seventeen or eighteen miles diagonally across the bay from us here.

The bay itself of which we are so proud is an ever-fresh ranging-ground for the eye, a wide expanse of almost Mediterranean blue on a clear day. On the opposite shore the slightly blurred effect that distance gives to the rugged cliff-contours and the few sloping fields that are visible over there, lends an extra beauty to the view as the colours on them change as the sun moves across the sky.

There is always a variety of movement on the sea itself; the large ocean-going vessels moving slowly way out along the wide horizon-line of the Atlantic, often half hidden under it; the smaller craft of the coastal trade close in to us; the daily crossing between Penzance and the Scilly Isles; the local boats of different build and size going to and from their fishing grounds; day by day the white foam striking from their bows as they cut at speed across the general and more widespread movement of the waves; the vague and rather exquisite feeling that there is more in what we see than meets the eye, real and beautiful though that is, a deeper and wider perception in ourselves perhaps of the mysterious nature of the world in which we live and of man's adventurous spirit in his relationship with it.

Fishing boats under sail are a spectacle of the past; but now that sailing for pleasure has become fashionable, we can watch the yacht

In Answer to the Cry

races in the summer, a hundred graceful little craft stretched out along their course. They are all 'laid up', however, before the winter storms begin. Even the larger trading vessels will change course and come in to greater safety then. A score or more will be riding at anchor at the head of the bay, sheltering especially from the fierce north-westerly gales.

At such times too birds not often seen in Cornwall will appear in the calmer stretches of water. They often escaped notice in the past, but in these days when there are so many competent bird-watchers about many of them are seen and identified. Mostly they come from further north and are never in large companies, often only a single bird. Among those recorded in 1976 in Mount's Bay alone were the black-throated, the great northern and the red-throated divers; the great-crested, the red-necked, the black-necked, Slavonian and little grebes; the velvet scoter, Merganser and goosander; the Brent and Canada geese; the grey phalarope and the great Arctic skuas. There were still others no doubt that were not recorded, and of course the birds of the storm itself, especially the shearwaters, or 'cleavers' as they are called locally, hurdling to left and right over the waves, and the little storm petrels, 'Mother Carey's chickens', half flying and half running along the heaving smoothness of a ship's wake near the stern. One or more of them were seen in Mousehole harbour a short time ago, and some of these rarer visitors sadly become patients at the hospital.

Westwards from here on our side of the bay the coast curves round in a rough semi-circle to Land's End ten or a dozen miles away. Except for a few coves where the longer valley streams have worn down an easy gradient to the sea it is a largely uninhabited area whose precipitous granite cliffs and headlands are backed by stretches of gorse and heather interspersed with bracken and bramble and thickets of stunted thorn. This uncultivated terrain has attracted a distinct bird life of its own. There are breeding colonies of gulls of different species, among them the kittiwakes, crowding the cliff faces where their nesting places are, afloat in the

The Birds of the Village

clear and boulder-strewn water of the inaccessible coves, or flying to and fro above them in all the irregular inter-headland hollows. Shags, too, are almost everywhere. Their laboured flight scarcely holds them above the surface of the water and many of the higher shore rocks are sprayed a permanent white, like snow, with their droppings.

The fulmar petrel that first established itself on this coast only thirty or forty years ago nests in close proximity to the gulls, and it is a pleasure to look down on its effortless flight as it glides swiftly along on its short 'aeroplane' wings, following the indentations of the coastline. Occasionally one can watch the buoyant, graceful, springing flight of a tern, its head and bill pointing straight down as it quarters the inshore water for fish below. The gannet never seems to come in to rest upon the rocks, but from these cliffs on windy days you can see a whole flock of them diving for fish a mile or two offshore, looking whiter out there in the stormy grey atmosphere than the white horses on the driving sea below. Those rapid, perpendicular dives of our largest sea birds, starting perhaps from a hundred feet in the air, with their long bent-back wings closing just before the splash, are the most spectacular sight this coastline affords, especially sometimes when they have spotted a shoal of fish much closer in to the shore.

Jackdaws, too, are numerous in their much older home on the cliffs beyond here; the same species as our village friends but much wilder and hardier birds. They nest among the gulls and fight with them around the ledges and the caves. They have a marvellous flight control even in the stormiest weather, shooting straight up and down the steep gullies with a falcon-like speed and precision. Here too is the home of their larger cousin the raven. You can see its dark rather menacing shape on almost every headland and a pair of them will fly and croak around you watching your every movement all the time.

The kestrel is perhaps more often seen in these parts than elsewhere, and one or two buzzards will usually be circling overhead, disdaining the mobbing attacks of the different members of the crow family that seem to object to their presence here. Their numbers have sadly diminished of recent years because of the insecticides used so much in farming now and the almost total absence of rabbits that were once a rich source of food for them. But the hospital has just released one of the few remaining buzzards back to its home.

There are a few land birds, both nesting and passage migrants, that are as typical of this coastal district as the larger ones that belong to the sea. As you walk along, with your eyes perhaps out at sea or your thoughts elsewhere, a not unmusical clicking sound as of two small pebbles being struck together may suddenly bring you back to your immediate surroundings. It is the call of the stonechat as he flies around his nesting places or with a brief whizzing of his wings tries to keep his balance on the topmost point of a low bush, from which with a curiosity equal to your own he faces round and watches you as you pass by; a happy and active little bird, lovely in his black and white and bright chestnut plumage, and lovelier still when you see him against the background of the purple-flowering heather and the yellow gorse. The female will be near him too but she lacks his brilliant colour and is easily mistaken for the rarer whinchat that is only a passage migrant here.

During the spring and autumn migrations other birds can be briefly seen on passage. A reed or a marsh warbler skulks in the reed beds that grow over a hidden spring in one or two of the grass-clad hollows, and whitethroats stay and nest in close association with the chats. The silent wheatear keeps to the more open places, and the cuckoo flies from one eminence to another, while somewhere in between its own voracious offspring is being frantically fed by its poor little foster-mother, a tiny meadow pipit that is perhaps only a tenth of its size. Our resident woodpecker, the yaffle, with its loping, wavy flight is a common sight, for in the warmest and most sheltered places ants and other flying insects

The Birds of the Village

abound. Occasionally a twittering flock of linnets will sweep across the downs and here as everywhere swallows and swifts are flying to and fro, the latter one of the latest migrants to arrive and one of the first to leave. The commonest of our land birds mostly keep away from this wilder coastline and when they come they somehow seem strangely out of place.

The final stretch along the cliffs, especially on a fine sunny day when the gorse and heather are in bloom at the same time, must be one of the loveliest walks in England. One feels the same joy and well-being as the larks in full song overhead as one approaches Land's End – the most south-westerly point of Britain, with closer views of the Atlantic, the Wolf Rock and the Longships lighthouses, and twenty-five miles away on the south-western horizon the low, dark outlines of the Scilly Isles.

At this end of Cornwall where there is such a large concentration of birds there are bound to be many casualties and deaths among them, both on the rocks and in the fields, many of which will go unrecorded and unnoticed. But as long as our hospital can survive, those that are lucky enough to be found by some compassionate human being will find help and sanctuary with us.

IV
A Prickly One

One day in July 1962 Pog and I were called back into active service by a ring on our telephone. An anxious voice besought help, saying she was just about to go on holiday and went to her coal cellar to be greeted by a mother hedgehog with three very young babies resting beside her. 'Send them to us. We will do what we can,' we answered, and frantically got busy preparing a 'house' to keep them in for the night in our sitting-room.

When they arrived we picked up mother and babies in a bunch and put them on the nest of hay in the darkened end of the house we had ready. The other end had a patch of grass, pans of soft food and water. A few squeaks and squawks and then complete peace reigned.

In the morning we took a peep to see if they were still alive, and found mother out feeding well, the three babies trying to copy her *and a fourth* baby cuddled up in the bedroom end!

At the time this little family came we were reading the life of Stanley Spencer, the artist whose work had always intrigued us. So we thought we would 'christen' them from the book. 'Mother' of course became Mrs Spencer, the largest baby Stanley, the next in size his sister and brother, Annie and Will, and the tiny newcomer, Gilbert.

We kept them in the sitting-room for a week, as they had adapted so well to their new home, while we prepared a space under our birds' balcony, 9 feet by 7 feet, with door and

A Prickly One

wire-netting front. We called it Cookham after the real Stanley Spencer home. We covered the earth with short turf and made three houses out of packing cases, one end darkened for the 'bedroom', the other open to the run.

All the babies had grown by the end of the week, so we put little Gilbert with Mrs Spencer in the largest house, Stanley alone in the second house as he was now so big, and Annie and Will together in the third house; in the run a large shallow pan of water, a bowl of bread and milk and a pan of finely chopped raw meat, some sluice (insectivorous food) and digestive biscuits. The grass contained worms and woodlice. So we hoped something in this mixed diet would meet with Mrs Spencer's approval. This it did, and all kept to their own houses in a wonderful way. At night we heard them scampering about. Mrs Spencer corrected us on one point. We had omitted a lavatory and this she arranged in one corner of the run which the babies were taught to use, and we cleared it out when necessary to conform with Mrs Spencer's ideas on hygiene.

We always had a look at them in the evening and gave them fresh food. But one night in November no Spencers were to be seen. Next morning no food had been eaten, nor had the lavatory been used. Hibernation was taking its natural course. We put down food but it was never touched. We were a bit worried by the first week in March, four months later in the following year, at not having seen or heard anything of them, so we quietly looked into the 'bedrooms'. All the young ones were rolled up in balls of straw, Mrs Spencer still sleeping with Gilbert. We put down fresh food and on 6th March it had all gone in the morning, though we saw no signs of the family. On 1st April they were all out in the sun, looking very fit and happy. After a day or two we left the door open all the time and off they must have gone, though we did not see them depart. We did see them coming to the lawn each evening for the food and custard we always put there for them.

In May we caught sight of one of them, at midnight, but after that we saw no more of them. The first week in November, however, back comes one Spencer in to Cookham and we think it must be Annie because she goes straight to her own house and uses the lavatory as of old. She comes out to eat but returns to her house instead of going off to the garden, so finally we shut the door. A week later we see her carrying all the dry leaves, grass and straw from her bedroom into Mrs Spencer's house where she makes a beautiful nest and from then on sleeps there. Two weeks later hibernation has begun and lasts until the following April when she starts coming out at nights again and the food left for her is gone by the morning. In May we open the door of the run. She comes and goes but by June we see her no more. The last of the Spencers has rejoined the wild.

Ten years later an excited member of the sanctuary staff told me a family of hedgehogs had arrived the day before. A man had lit a bonfire and when it was well alight he was horrified to hear cries from within the blaze and discovered a mother hedgehog covering her six babies to protect them from the flames. He instantly put them in a box and brought them straight to the hospital. The little ones seemed unharmed but the mother, in spite of treatment, died in the night, probably of burns and shock. She had given her life for her children.

Without the comforting presence of her body the six orphans rapidly began to chill and one became terribly distressed. This smallest baby trotted ceaselessly in and out of their cardboard house, squealing pitifully for his mother just like a tiny piglet. It was clear a substitute source of heat had to be found and it was provided by a hot-water bottle wrapped in a piece of blanket. As soon as this was put in their house, the hedgehogs cuddled on to its warm surface, six little pin-cushions clustered together. All became peaceful once more.

These babies were much smaller than the Spencers and had to be fed with Ostermilk from a syringe, about one small teaspoon at a time. They soon got the idea of sucking from the narrow rubber

A Prickly One

tube that served as a nipple. They nestled into the palm of the hand, pressing hard down with their little feet as they tugged at their new food supply. Their liquid diet satisfied them for a while but after a week or so they objected to the syringe and were feeding themselves from the pan of more solid food we offered them. At about this time they began to resent being handled and if we touched them in cleaning out their cage, they jumped and squeaked and raced back into their house on sturdy little legs. Because their spines were hardening now this rejection of familiarities was mutually accepted.

They became named The Poggles and two weeks later, no longer in need of mother hot-water bottle, they were moved into a run of their own, with a large house, one end of which was dark and filled with hay for their bedroom. They loved it and it was called Buckingham Palace. They grew apace, and so another house (with bedroom) was made and called Balmoral. They split up of their own accord, three living in Buckingham Palace and three in Balmoral. However, as no lavatory had been provided, they were forced finally to use Balmoral for this purpose, and all crowded back into the Palace.

By this time they were getting enormous, so another even bigger house was made of which they were graciously pleased to approve, except for the bedding, however. They scampered about and tore up the carpet of newpapers into shreds and with the hay contrived a new bed which pleased them greatly. At the end of the year there were no signs of hibernation. They continued to stay in their house by day and moved out each night, eating well. It had been an exceptionally mild winter, so perhaps that accounted for their activity. Now all were fully grown, perfectly fit and self-reliant and sometimes beginning to squabble amongst themselves. So in April they were taken to the fields and off they rushed to take their place in the wild world. A rewarding sight for the girls who had cared for them so well.

By now we were on such happy terms with the staff that we

In Answer to the Cry

always referred to them as 'the girls'. Their names were Olga Penrose, the warden, and her two assistants Peggy Bell and Pamela Baines. In the years since 1960 there had been several wardens and several changes of staff. But happily Olga, Peggy and Pamela are all still caring for the birds at the hospital today.

V
Charlie and Oliver

The longer the girls worked at the hospital the more fresh insight they experienced of the powerful individuality of the different birds and the delightful intricacies of their behaviour. Some birds pass through the hospital so quickly, either sadly through unavoidable death or happily through release, that they never acquire a personal name. They are our brief encounters. Some are so individual on arrival that they are immediately christened. And some acquire names as they remain in the hospital and their idiosyncrasies become all too apparent. Like those of the two rooks Charlie and Oliver, whose story Pam tells here:

   Charlie was brought seeking 'sanctuary' rather in the sense of a latter-day reprobate banging on a monastery door to escape retribution for his sins. He had been found as a baby and hand-reared by a family living not far away. Separated from his natural environment, this highly intelligent member of the crow family had adapted himself to his new life amongst human beings with remarkable ease. As he grew older curiosity begat confidence and Charlie began to look upon the house as a superior rookery and re-arrange it to his own taste. Anything that could be torn, was torn, everything that could be tippled over – tippled. He began to build 'nests' over the cooker, which created many a culinary disaster. When he learnt to fly his excursions into the outside world provided further opportunities to test the versatility of his busy beak. He discovered washing lines and quickly learnt that pegs on washing lines could be unpegged and what was more there were row upon row of them! Housewives did not appreciate Charlie's new skill.

With mounting complaints from the neighbours and the continuing chaos in their own home, his adopted family decided to bring him to the hospital for his own safety. At the end of his case history it seemed Charlie himself tried to say a few words in his own defence but they were unintelligible. In fact they would have been of little consequence. It took him several months to perfect 'Come on' and 'Good morning'. And such was the effort over these four words that they became the total range of his human vocabulary.

We joined him up with more sober members of his race in their run where, over the next couple of years, his buoyant nature and perfect physical condition carried him to the top of the pecking order in the little community. Visitors were captivated by his sociable 'Good Mornings', – no matter if it might be afternoon – and those who made an annual pilgrimage to the hospital would immediately enquire, 'Is Charlie still here?' Children especially loved him and would stand beside the run encouraging him to talk. Sometimes they got the salutation wrong.

'Hello. Hello. Hello,' they would repeat with parrot-like persistency.

'Good morning. Good morning. Come on,' he used to correct with equal fervour.

In the spring of his second year Charlie decided the time had come for him to choose a mate. He courted Shadrack, a rook who had been with us a year longer. She had been brought in with her right wing shattered by shot-gun pellets. The break had set awkwardly and she became a permanent resident. It would have taken a strong-minded rook to reject the handsome Charlie. Not only did he bring presents of cheese and biscuits but he also spiced his wooing by standing on the edge of the nest box in ritual display

Charlie and Oliver

and, with a seductive twinkle in his eye, would entice her to enter with an enthusiastic 'Come on! Come on!'

Their marriage lasted for four years during which time he proved himself a most faithful and attentive husband to the rather cantankerous Shadrack. She much preferred the excitement of courtship to the mundane business of egg hatching each year, after about a fortnight's sitting, the empty green and brown blotched shells would be found smashed on the ground below the nest. In the autumn of their fourth year together Shadrack became the victim of coccidosis, a particularly virulent form of enteritis. She was brought inside for treatment, rallied for a month but failed again and died, leaving Charlie a youthful widower.

The following spring he chose another mate and they settled down together. It looked as though he had found happiness again, but the next year there entered upon the scene a youthful 'Jezebel' who broke all social conventions and brazened her way into his affections. Her name was Oliver.

In the year of Shadrack's death, Oliver had been found walking up a street in Penzance. She was small, rather weak and *very* tame. Someone had probably found her as a baby and tried to rear her. Whether they had lost interest in her or whether Oliver herself had decided to see a bit more of the world we did not know. However, she came to the sanctuary and after being put on a high protein diet, began to thrive. She soon asserted herself to being 'first at the table', so to speak, and wolfed down all she could, still squawking for more, even with her beak full. And so she received her somewhat inappropriately masculine name of Oliver Twist. Within a short time she was fit enough to join the older rooks in The Nancy Price run* and there she passed her first year, becoming a little more independent, but always first in line for any tit-bits that might be had.

By the spring of her second year, Oliver, though still rather undersized, was in beautiful condition. Her glossy black feathers

*So named after the actress who took such an interest in the hospital.

sheened with blues and purples as she flirted amongst her companions. It was now that Charlie noticed her for the first time. The wife he had chosen to replace his beloved Shadrack had none of the advantages of her capricious rival. She was very retiring and, like Shadrack, had a terrible wing injury — perhaps this is what had attracted Charlie?

At any rate he became besotted with Oliver but he was torn by loyalty to his true wife, feeding first one and then the other as he tried to choose between them. Finally he came to a compromise and set up house with Oliver, who was a shamelessly adoring mistress. But he still continued to take tender presents to his spouse.

The 'love-nest' began to take shape. Charlie would bring the twigs and sticks and proudly put them into the nest box. Oliver, looking on with excitement, would finally go and inspect his work. She would promptly pull out the carefully placed furnishings and drop them to the ground, as much as to say 'Not quite right, dear'. After much to-ing and fro-ing Oliver was at last satisfied and settled on to the now very large nest with the harassed Charlie standing guard.

When Oliver laid her three eggs her femininity was proved but the diminuation of her name to 'Olive' somehow did not fit and so Oliver she remained. She quickly grew bored with her role as mother and though Charlie began to take his turn sitting on the eggs this solution suited Oliver no better. One day, as soon as he came off the nest, she jumped in and broke every egg. The nest which had been built with such care was demolished, and as the heat of summer passed so too did passions cool. Charlie forsook his mistress and turned again to his long-suffering mate. Oliver did not seem to object to this arrangement until another breeding season came round.

Charlie had decided that running a harem was too exhausting and made it clear that he had no intention of renewing their liaison. No amount of coquetry on Oliver's part could weaken his

Charlie and Oliver

resolve and so, true to the tradition that 'hell hath no fury like a woman scorned', she set about revenging herself on Charlie's mate. When domestic squabbling deteriorated to a bloody battle between the two rivals, we were forced to remove her to a separate pen. It was not hard to sympathise with this sad victim of unrequited love. Oliver's feelings for Charlie had been very deep and pathetically she built herself a lonely nest, then sat on it gazing over to Charlie. Charlie, too, was to suffer loss that year. He became a widower for the second time when his 'wife' died quite suddenly. He seemed to have no desire to make a new attachment and because of this we decided to try and release him, hoping for the best.

Charlie was in perfect condition and the delinquent days of his youth were ancient history. We were loathe to let him go but the time seemed right, so we opened the door and watched him fly off. After that he returned each day to the hospital for several months, cawing to his old companions. To our relief Oliver never took any notice of him. Gradually Charlie came back less and less until, finally all contact was broken and we never saw him again.

Meanwhile Oliver had become 'Queen' of the rooks' run but she, too, now was a perfectly healthy bird and, governed by the success of Charlie's release, we decided to give her the same chance of freedom. When first let out, she stayed on top of the run all day and in the evening was waiting by the gate to come in. This became a daily routine. With confidence growing she flew further afield but always within sight of the hospital. She often visited Pog at her studio window, demanding food, and would return with a beak full of cheese and biscuits, which she generously offered around to the staff. Still returning each night to be 'put to bed', she would call for the gate of the run to be opened. Later she learnt how to unhook the latch herself and began to let herself in of her own accord.

Unfortunately, although proficient at opening her door, Oliver had not learnt to close it and to prevent her convalescing friends from getting out we had to remove the hook and jam the gate. This done she now had to call us again each evening to be let in. Not to be thwarted, Oliver found she could unhook all the other gates. Fortunately this caused few problems as they did not swing open as easily as her own. Hooks certainly held a fascination for her and in time she also discovered how to *close* them, much to the consternation of Peggy. While cleaning out the deep pond inside a pen one day, she was shut in by Oliver and imprisoned for nearly an hour before her cries for help were heard.

Oliver relished the coming of summer. Always companionable, she would join us at our coffee break and bask in the sunshine, wings ecstatically spread and beak wide open. This was a somewhat disconcerting sight for the visitors who did not realise her agonised looking pose was typical of a bird enjoying the sun. Her morning visits were not always so blissfully inactive, though. She could move like lightning and cries of 'Oh Oliver' would follow her as she dunked her biscuits in a half-drunk cup of coffee or unrolled her own cigarette from any packet left within her reach. Her attentions were not directed solely at us. Once she confiscated a packet of crisps out of the hand of a visitor. But her most infamous exploit was when she swooped down from the sky and, without pausing in flight, lifted a chocolate flake bar out of an ice cream. She left the girl holding the cone with a startled look of amazement on her face and a gaping hole in the ice.

To enlarge her business of the day, she began to accompany Olga as she took her little daughter to school. This became an almost unfailing morning duty and, in time, she improved upon it with her own set of rituals. On the open spaces of Raginnis Hill, below the hospital, she would go on foot, but, as the street narrowed at the bottom and passed through the village, she soared up into the air and flew above the roof-tops until the street widened again near the school. There she alighted on the gate and waited for Olga to say goodbye to Linda before repeating the journey homeward. This went on for some time and then, quite suddenly, the pattern was broken. Instead of coming straight back to the hospital, Oliver began to make reconnaissance flights towards a small rookery behind the school. There are so few tall trees around the village in this windy part of the country, that the rooks had quickly commandeered these welcome high branches. It is well known that by preference they nest in elms, and the Dutch elm disease which has overtaken most of the country must have robbed many of their homes. But the Mousehole rooks are beggars who cannot be choosers and make do with what they can find.

This new diversion in Oliver's flight path began to occupy more and more of her time. Later she missed out her school visit all together and soon she was spending whole days on end away from the hospital. She remained with us through another winter, torn between the security of the hospital and the new life that she had discovered with the wild rooks. Then when the weather started to warm at last, she again took to leaving us for a few days at a time. The days away lengthened to weeks and the only sign of an occasional visit 'home' was when we went out to find all the gate hooks undone. Finally, even this ceased. But we knew she was safe. One of the girls who used to work at the hospital lives near the rookery and Oliver had recognised her and started to pay her the occasional visit. It seemed she still was not prepared to sever the links between herself and the humans who had been so much a part of her life.

Very few of the birds stay with us for as long as Charlie and Oliver, yet some can be remembered with almost equal affection and, sometimes, not without their moments of humour. Their characterful personalities very often fill the gap left by a long-term patient or break a quiet spell in the life of the hospital. But there are very few quiet spells, and these rare times usually come in the early winter months and they are not without their compensations. It is a time for repainting cages or giving the guillemot house a floor to ceiling scrub in preparation for the oiled seabirds which we

In Answer to the Cry

know will come our way before very long. The only thing we cannot predict is whether they will number a hundred in a 'good' year — if there can be such a thing — or a thousand in a bad.

It was nearing Christmas, during one such quiet spell, that a large, pure white, Muscovy duck was found waddling down a street in Newlyn, the fishing port a few miles away. She was brought to the hospital and we informed the local police about Tabitha, as we had christened her, because being a domesticated duck she must have had an owner somewhere. However, no one came to claim her and so we decided to give her story to *The Cornishman* newspaper in the hopes that this would attract someone's attention. *The Cornishman* co-operated and put in an amusing little feature about the 'duck who will not become a Christmas dinner'.

The next day a girl arrived to claim Tabitha and it transpired that the story in the paper had been all too near the truth. Fourteen of her Muscovy ducks had been stolen one night and only Tabitha had escaped. She must have felt lonely so took off on her own in search of her companions. Anyway, now reunited with her owner, she departed and we assumed that this would be the happy conclusion to her story.

A week later, at six o'clock in the morning, a policeman on patrol in a panda car saw Tabitha once more waddling down a Newlyn street. She was promptly arrested and brought back to us. Her owner was once more informed and, when we explained to her that Tabitha would continue to wander unless she had company, she asked us if we would look after her as she was obviously unhappy on her own.

This presented us with something of a problem because we felt that whilst we could undertake to care for the duck this was not the ideal solution to her loneliness. We wanted to find her a new home where she would have company of her own kind. As so often happens, through a chance conversation with one of our friends such a place was found with bird lovers living close to Praa Sands.

Charlie and Oliver

The day for Tabitha's arrival at her new home was agreed upon and she travelled over one lovely, sunny afternoon. Her new address was located and, from the moment we entered the drive, it was clear that Tabitha had landed in clover. In large, beautifully constructed aviaries, white peacocks perched on thick branches, their glorious tails like cascading waterfalls nearly touched the ground. Near the house more peacocks, of iridescent blue, were busy patrolling the paths. At the far end of an almost lawn-like field, the ducks and geese who were to be Tabitha's new companions congregated around and upon a stretch of deepish stream. In the middle of the stream was a small, round island and floating among the reeds by the bank was an enormous Moscovy drake.

Tabitha strolled out of her basket and shook herself free of travel cramp. Then she spotted the drake. Her feathers fluffed and she eagerly waddled down the bank to make his acquaintance. With necks outstretched they met each other on the water, the drake was as white as Tabitha herself — a perfectly matched pair.

Alas, the sight of so much quivering duckliness was too much for the drake. His crest rose on end and his passions flamed to match the crimson of the knobbly flesh around his bill. Tabitha, suddenly realising that her new-found friend's intentions were not entirely honourable, began to back paddle frantically. In a desperate effort to save her virtue she tried to dodge behind the island but the drake pursued her remorselessly. Round and round the little hummock of reed and grass they went until at last poor Tabby was overwhelmed by her lover in a flurry of feathers and much splashing of water. It seemed a trifle unkind that she should have escaped an untimely end as a Christmas dinner, only to meet a Fate worse than Death on a stream at Praa Sands. However, there was no doubt as to which state Tabitha preferred to be in. After a bit she composed her feathers and glided off in the wake of her lord and master to join him in a triumphal progress down the stream.

VI
Badgers and Seals

Like the Prickly Ones, not all our patients are feathered. Some come furred, the badgers for instance that the hospital cared for several years ago. Untypical of many English counties, Cornwall's badger population is, as yet, not endangered. The moors and rough coastland have provided the perfect breeding grounds for Brock. The badgers we have had were admitted within the space of two years and the first of them taught us that there is still much truth in the adage, 'where there is life there is hope'. Her name was Louisa. Pam tells what happened.

It was late on a very wet and stormy October evening that the young sow badger was brought to the hospital. She had been found by a man at the side of the road, half a dozen miles away. He carried her up the steep steps in a stout wooden crate and, after a bed of straw had been hastily shaken down in one of the empty bird houses, he gently tipped her on to the ground. Still barely conscious, the badger instinctively pushed her way under the straw. Before she vanished it could be seen that a wide patch of fur had been skinned off her back and her hind legs appeared to be totally useless. She had obviously been hit by a car as she set off on her evening search for food.

The following morning a veterinary surgeon was called out to see her. Louisa, as she had been named, was by this time mentally alert and very frightened. As gently as possible, her shivering body was extricated from the straw and manoeuvered against the wall

The Spirit of Flame.   *The Man Alive.*

Wood sculpture by Pog.

Pog at her studio window, carving.

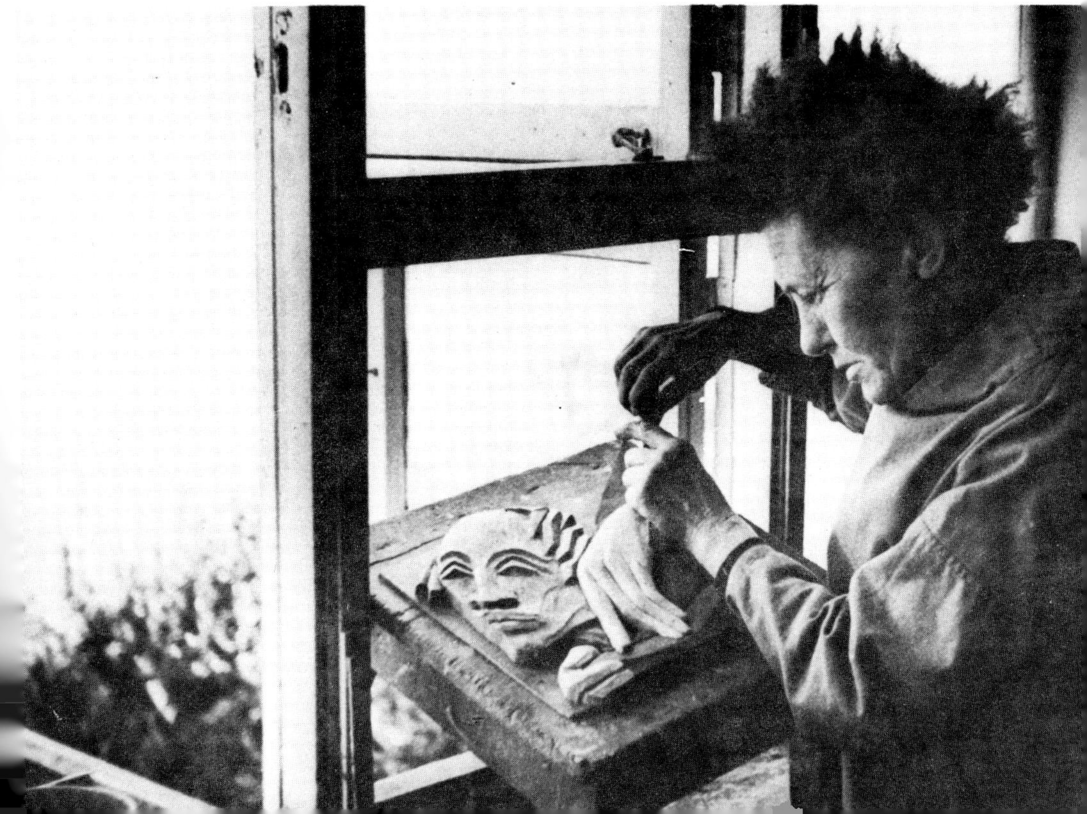

Oiled swans from the Falmouth river, later released where found.

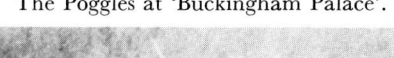

The Poggles at 'Buckingham Palace'.

A sick shag.

Guillemots inspecting their quarters.

Louisa the badger, finding her legs again.
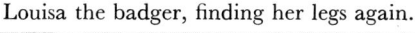

Albert Ross, young greater blackbacked gull. Proud of his new feathers, he arrived with very bad plumage.

Oliver, the rook.

Our reward – the trust of a wild bird.

with a frame of wire mesh. Through this the vet was able to inject her with antibiotics and tranquilliser. She was heavily sedated and after a lengthy examination was found to not only have completely dislocated both hips, but had also broken her right foreleg. The wound on her back was superficial and her left leg unharmed. The vet prescribed that time and nature be given a chance to heal her damaged limbs, though this could take anything up to six weeks or longer.

His advice to keep her as immobile as possible was not hard to follow. With only one fit leg she was unable to move anyway. We fed her on a diet of dog biscuits, raw meat and egg, and placed her food bowl within nose-reach of her bed. Water, too, was provided.

Louisa proved to be a model patient, although at first she used to make angry coughing grunts when she was gently rolled, with a broom, from her bed so that we could remove the soiled straw. She gradually came to tolerate her 'nurses' and we, in turn, respected the trust she showed. For there is a sense of privilege in being so close to a creature of the wild.

A week went by and then a fortnight and still she showed no sign of regaining the use of her back legs. During the second week she developed enteritis, which must have been terribly distressing for an animal as fastidious as the badger because she could not help fouling herself and her bed. Kaobiotic was added to her drinking water and after seven days the condition responded to treatment.

The third week came and went without her attempting to walk, though her broken foreleg showed signs of taking some weight. We began to wonder if we were doing the right thing by continuing with her and yet she was eating well and her eyes were bright, not those of a desperately sick animal. Then one morning Louisa was gently 'broomed' out of bed as usual. She half-rolled on to the floor and her hind legs, instead of dragging uselessly behind, came up beneath her body. She remained perfectly still for a few moments then shuffled a few, unsteady steps forward . . . she was using both hind legs.

In Answer to the Cry

From that day onward, she made slow but sure progress to recovery. She was so used to the daily cleaning out routine that, as soon as she saw us, she would climb out of her bed and with ever strengthening steps would wander into the outside run while we tidied up her 'bedroom'. When we put her food in last thing at night we would find her blissfully asleep on her back. Her black and white snout rested on front paws folded comfortably across the dark fur of her stomach, with her hind legs stretched out luxuriously in front of her. Round ears twitched at the scrape of her food bowl on the floor and beady eyes opened to regard us with lazy confidence.

It was not until the new year, however, that talk began about releasing her. By this time she had had her photo and story published in *The Cornishman*. It was through this article that we were able to re-contact the young man who had originally found her. He promised that when the time came he he would take us and Louisa close to the place where she had been injured so that she could be released in 'home' territory.

Our decision to release her was precipitated by signs that she was no longer content with her life at the hospital. Splinters of wood found in the outside run told a tale of determined gnawing. Soon after, close neighbours somewhat nervously enquired what had we got here, because they were disturbed nightly by a terrible rattling and banging. Then Louisa began to leave her food. Her wild spirit was pining for freedom and the time had come for her to leave us.

She had her 'all clear' from the vet and her rescuer was telephoned. He agreed to help with her release the following evening, weather permitting.

Nothing could have been more perfect than that January night. The young man arrived about nine-thirty, carrying the same crate in which he had brought her to us all those weeks ago. But Louisa was a far cry from the miserable, helpless creature of that day. She dashed into the outside run and with the effortlessness of a little bear, she shinned up the wire meshing to roof height, clinging on with her powerful rooting claws. With a little difficulty, she was crated up, the top was secured and she was carried down the steps to her waiting transport.

We followed our guide on a drive of several miles to a piece of open countryside where, beyond a large field, moorland stretched away into the distance. The young man carried her crate several hundred yards down a wide earth track and we walked on behind. The air was so crisp it stung our nostrils and the near full moon in a cloudless sky lit our way. When we felt we were far enough from the road, the crate was placed on the ground and the top removed. For maybe a minute or more Louisa hesitated inside. The crate was tipped a little and at last she emerged. The moment the badger's paws felt the turf beneath them she was away. In the moonlight we could see her small grey shape scurrying into the distance and heard her making quiet chuttering cries that were carried back on the still air even after she had gone from sight.

Then there was only silence. The empty crate was picked up and we too went home.

It was only a matter of four months before we met our second badger. He was brought to us by the RSPCA Inspector and had been found on the north coast in a very weak condition. This boar badger was a complete contrast to the pretty, feminine Louisa. He was much battle-scarred, with both ears torn off. He earned his name Pongo simply because he stank.

Pongo had evidently come off second best in his most recent tussle and was badly gashed about his neck and back. The wounds had become infected and the poison seemed likely to have begun to spread through his body.

A young vet came out to treat the badger's wounds and through lessons learnt from our dealings with Louisa, we soon had Pongo pinned against the wall for his injections of antibiotic and tranquilliser. It was hoped that when he was comatose we would be able to clean out his sores. But 'enough drug to lay a donkey out' was not sufficient to floor a battler like Pongo. He remained steadfastly conscious and so his wounds had to stay unattended.

Another vet called the following day and this time Pongo submitted to the injection and the necessary treatment. As had been feared, the infection was widespread and the vet told us he would visit again in a few days to check on Pongo's progress. According to our 'medical diary' the badger must have been making a good recovery because on this third visit no further injections were needed and only wound powder had to be put on the sores.

Pongo remained in our care for a month and, like Louisa, stoically accepted hospitalisation while he regained his strength. In time all his scars healed and he was fighting fit again when we released him near a vacant badger sett not far away.

The next occasion that we had to treat a badger was under far less happy circumstances. This new patient was only a youngster and had been found on a housing estate in Penzance. It was in a very sickly condition and was believed to have eaten poison. In spite of immediate veterinary attention the little badger was too far gone for help.

It is said that things happen in threes and so we almost expected that this would be our last encounter with these animals. But we were proved wrong. A few months later yet another stripey-faced patient was settling down in its straw bed to await veterinary inspection. Like Louisa, it had been found by the roadside, evidently another 'hit and run' victim. However, although there was slight grazing at the base of its spine, it was otherwise uninjured and mildly concussed. Five days later it trotted off into the undergrowth near to the place where it had been found.

Strangely, we have never treated another badger since that time, but the memories of our contact with these fascinating creatures still live on. In fact, any badger we treated now for whatever reason would have to be tested for bovine TB, of which they are sometimes carriers, before it was released back into the wild.

Badgers and Seals

We also have had links with that furred creature of the sea, the Atlantic or grey seal, that breeds in small colonies around these coasts. The cow seal gives birth to its young in mid-September, well above high-tide level and the beautiful little calf has a thick coat of creamy-white fur. For three weeks it remains on land, suckling the cow's rich milk and putting on weight at the rate of nearly four pounds a day, until it is bloated with fat. At three weeks the baby fur is cast for a sleek, sea-going coat of slightly mottled, grey, short hairs. The baby seal is about to become a 'weaner' and takes to the water with its mother. Soon she no longer feeds it and the baby has to live off its store of fat until it reaches almost starvation level when hunger drives it to catch its own food.

It is at this point in its life that the little seal is at its weakest and therefore most vulnerable. Sometimes battered by a fierce winter gale, it is washed ashore and left by the receding tide. This is the time when we might receive a phone call that begins, 'Can you help, there's a seal lying on the beach . . . '

The seals we tried to save in the early years were of varying size and age. The youngest were generally very weak, suffering from malnutrition and lung conditions. Most had their sea-going coats but one or two were still baby-furred. Their stay with us was usually short and had sad endings. Although every care was taken with them, we were unable to feed them correctly. They always appeared so sad and inconsolable, with their huge, pathetic, dark eyes that seemed perpetually on the point of tears. Their cries were really heartbreaking, a pitifully bawled, 'Maa! Maa!'

The largest seal we ever looked after came into our care late one evening. It was fully grown and had been found stranded in the river near Gweek, a tidal creek in the Helford district about twenty miles away, on the other side of the Lizard peninsula. The seal had been rescued by the RSPCA Inspector and his wife and it was so massive that a cry for help went out to bring it up the hospital steps. It took eight volunteers to carry it up to the Guillemot House. It must have weighed several hundredweight and seemed almost to fill the small inner room. Sadly when the vet examined it he found it to be totally blind in both eyes and, since it could not be released in that state, it had to be humanely destroyed.

However, we were not without our successes. One day we got a message from some fishermen that a young seal had been washed up at Penberth Cove, some miles westward along the coast from here. Three of us went out to pick it up and found we had to abandon the car in the lane nearly half a mile from the beach. Torrential rain had caused flooding and we found ourselves walking down a swift running 'river' about halfway up our wellington boots. The seal turned out to be the most obese youngster we had ever seen. The fishermen had put it in a huge wooden box and took it up the road for us on the back of a lorry which was high enough to negotiate the flooding rain-water.

Fat Freda, as we named this seal, had several cuts about the face and body and we treated these with antiseptic cream. But otherwise she was unharmed and in view of her general fitness, we decided to release her as soon as the weather settled. She was duly returned to the sea after being with us only a couple of days.

Just four days after Fat Freda's departure, yet another seal was reported in trouble, this time on the Mousehole rocks. We went down to investigate and found a nearly half-grown seal on the beach, plastered with thick oil. We rolled it up in sacks, somehow got it in the boot of the car and brought it back to the hospital. By this time our new patient was in a fury. With its body fat rippling at every movement, it 'lumped' towards us with surprising speed on its flat flippers. We decided discretion was the better part of valour and asked the vet to come and give the seal a mild sedative before we began to clean off the oil. To make the procedure even safer we muzzled it as well. The gaping pink of its open mouth was studded with an impressive set of teeth which we had found a rather intimidating sight.

Even in its slightly sleepy condition, the seal did not take too kindly to our ministrations. It squirmed and puffed and snorted as

Badgers and Seals

we worked an oil emulsifying cream into its coat. Fortunately we were able to remove all the oil in one cleansing and afterwards the seal rinsed itself in the pond, blowing contemptuous bubbles at us as it wallowed about in the water. By the next morning it was so obstreperous that it was taken off later that day to a safe beach, where it wasted no time in putting as much sea as possible between itself and its releaser.

Already, in the year of writing, we have given brief shelter to two baby seals, left as pathetic, round-eyed jetsam on Mousehole beaches. One we went down to pick up ourselves and the other, two local ladies had found. Showing great ingenuity, they had managed to get the little seal in a wheelbarrow and pushed it 'in state' through the village, where we met it with more conventional transport to take it the rest of the way to the hospital. On such occasions we are still quite happy to act as a 'resting house' for these sick youngsters but we know our limitations. A valuable contact has been made with Mr Ken Jones of The Cornish Seal Sanctuary and now our seals are sent on to him as soon as possible for his expert care.

VII
Newcomers to the Hospital

From the beginning the most frequent patients Pog and I had to deal with at the hospital were jackdaws, gulls, sea birds, garden birds and birds of prey, but over the past few years the girls have also received many unusual birds at the sanctuary, some of which they now describe:

One of the most unusual ones was a Demoiselle crane found wandering on a golf course. Whilst these birds can be vagrant visitors to the British Isles, it was obvious from its clipped wings and calm behaviour that our new guest must have strayed from a private aviary. He was put in the gulls' big run and was soon tucking into a feed of corn and maize. The police were informed and a photo and an article about him appeared in a local newspaper in the hope that his owner could be traced.

While with us he spent most of his time standing statue-still with his head and beak tucked so tightly into his chest that the long black feathers of his neck hung down, just like a cloak, around the grey of his body. He peered at us with bright red eyes, behind each of which sprouted a tuft of white feathers and he looked very stern indeed, and very like a judge, which is the name he was given. When The Judge decided to take a rare break from the pressures of 'court sessions' he would pace the run with measured, slow-motion strides. It would have been interesting to know what the gulls made of their exotic companion.

Newcomers to the Hospital

In spite of all the publicity given him no one claimed The Judge and so enquiries were made to zoos within reasonable travelling distance to see if a new home could be found for him. Luckily Ilfracombe Zoo, some hundred miles away on the North Devon coast, offered to take him and so, after a few more days' rest, he was transported there and we later heard that he had stood the journey well and was settled and content.

Then there was the little egret blown exhausted aboard a fishing boat thirty-two miles off the Lizard. Unfortunately it died after a few days here from an infection of the air sacs, which was probably the reason for it having been blown off course in the first place.

Another 'first-timer' was a nightjar. It had been kept for a week before it was sent to us and its badly injured wing showed signs of a deep-seated infection. These strange birds are summer visitors and are rarely seen, mainly because they fly at dusk or after dark, feeding on moths and beetles. By day they rest motionless on the ground, their soft plumage a miracle of camouflage with its subtle blend of grey, autumn shades and black.

Our nightjar's feeding habits presented us with a dreadful problem. We caught every moth in sight, chopped up meal worms and shredded raw meat into minute pieces. The bird had to be force-fed. It came as quite a shock to find that when the tiny beak was gently prised open, an enormous frog-like gaping mouth was revealed. The sides of the mouth were fragile and the lower part was like a film of clouded cellophane which nature had made sticky to become a perfect insect trap.

In spite of all that could be done the nightjar never looked like responding to treatment. After only a few days it died peacefully in its sleep, which was of small consolation to us.

Usually, like the nightjar, our patients arrive in ones but sometimes they come in a crowd. One September, over a period of three days, thirty-one Manx shearwaters were admitted to the hospital. This was an unusually large number. We usually get only perhaps five throughout a normal year. They were all found on the

In Answer to the Cry

estuary beach at Hayle, near St Ives and a dozen miles from us. Most of them were brought by the local RSPCA Inspector; others by visitors. The weather had been misty for several days and the shearwaters had probably become lost and exhausted on migration. They were put in an empty section of the pigeon loft where they scurried into the darkest corner. As new arrivals came they rushed to join the others, with slender bills outstretched and soon became lost in the growing mass of black and white feathers. During the day they were quite silent but as dusk fell they could be heard scuttling about on the wooden floor, crooning to each other. In the wild, on their breeding grounds, they become nocturnal in habit and no doubt the darkened loft seemed a substitute for the burrows they live in.

Though half were lost, perhaps due to complete exhaustion, the others recovered and after a few days' rest were ready to be returned to the wild. At twilight they were carried down in baskets to the rocky beach below the hospital. One after another they were launched into the air and away they went, skimmimg the waves to freedom.

One Guy Fawkes Day, some years later, another unusual patient came into our care. We received a phone call from people living in St Mary's over on the Scilly Isles. They had found 'a strange looking swan' which they believed had been shot. Could they send it over to us for treatment? To this we instantly agreed but the problem remained of transporting the swan to the mainland.

The Scillies are the group of islands and islets which rise out of the Atlantic some twenty-eight miles west of Land's End. They are famous for their early spring flowers and the rare tropical plants which grow on one of them. In the calm of summer the sea around their shores is sparkling clear and blinding white beaches soak up the heat of the sun. The smaller islands and rocky outcrops are uninhabitable to man, but they provide a haven for breeding colonies of puffins, terns, shearwaters, gulls and other sea birds.

So that the swan could reach us with the least possible delay, it

Newcomers to the Hospital

was decided not to send it by sea. This trip takes two and a half hours from Hugh Town to Penzance and to say that it can be 'very choppy' is an understatement. Besides, the *Scillonian*, the boat which plies between the mainland and the islands, was now on winter service and not making its usual return journey each day. So instead arrangements were made to fly the bird over in the BEA helicopter. The blue and white liveried Sikorsky makes light of the distance between St Mary's and Penzance but what the swan thought about mechanical flight is a speculative matter. It was carried across the tarmac in the largest dog travelling crate that could be found and must have been almost deafened by the noise of the engine and the frantic whirling of the rotor-blades as they became a spinning haze. The flight which might have provided a familiar experience to the swan, with the aerial view of sea and coastline was spent in harsh, vibrating semi-darkness.

We collected the bird from the Heliport on the outskirts of Penzance and brought it in the crate back to the hospital. When it was taken out we saw that it was indeed a 'strange looking swan'. Although equally as large as the Mute variety we knew so well, it more resembled a giant goose. It had a thick-set body and a very stiffly upright neck; there were bold yellow markings on its bill. We decided from its huge size that the swan was of the Whooper species and later confirmed this from our books. Whoopers are winter visitors, chiefly to Scotland and Wales. They breed in and near the Arctic regions of Northern Europe and Russia. In spite of its bulk, the swan had a rather feminine appearance and we called her Hope.

She was in a state of deep shock and had lost complete use of her legs. Yet she still made wild lunges to get away from us by using her wings as crutches. We put her in the quiet and warmth of the Guillemot House and the vet was called out to examine her. He concurred with the suspicion that Hope had been shot and although her left wing was not broken it was very hot and swollen and the underside had been opened almost to the bone. This

1975　　　　**September**

Saturday　　　　**6**
249–116
s.r. 6.20, s.s. 7.36

D /	Young Housemartin (ADM 4 9 75) found dead AM	D 543
D /	Young Housemartin (ADM 1 9 75) found dead AM	D 543
A852 /	HAWFINCH (D 7.9.75) NEWLYN INJURED BY CAT.	
A853 /	YOUNG BLACKBIRD (D 8.9.75) MOUSEHOLE CAUGHT BY CAT	
R /	MALLARD DUCK (AD)	√ ~~263~~ 271
R /	" " " (A.D.) RELEASED HAYLE RIVER.	√ ~~264~~ 272
R /	SHEERWATER (AD 1. 9. 75)	√ ~~265~~ 273
R /	" " " (AD. 1. 9. 75) R AT GODREAVY	√ 266 274
R /	GANNET (AD 30. 8. 75) R AT GODREAVY	√ ~~267~~ 275
R /	PIDGEON ( )	√ ~~268~~ 276
R /	" ( )	√ ~~269~~ 277
R /	" ( )	√ ~~270~~ 278
R /	" ( )	√ ~~271~~ 279
A854 /	S/HAWK (D 4 9.75.) PERRONUTHNOE CONCUSSED. OFF LEGS	

A typical entry from the hospital records. The spread wing sign indicates release.

wound was several inches long and 'weeping' badly. Hope was given an antibiotic injection to counteract the infection. We strapped a protective pad over the injured wing to prevent further damage should she start battering and at last were able to leave her in peace to recover from her ordeals.

The next morning we found her calmer but she had not touched her feed of chick crumb mash. She had passed some foul, dark green droppings which indicated the emptiness of her stomach and the beginnings of enteritis. We dosed her as a precaution against the latter. While one of us held her still, another dribbled the medicine past the side of her rough tongue and down her throat. This added indignity could not have helped endear us to her.

Indeed, over the next four days it began to look as though Hope had lost all will to survive. She no longer panicked at our approach and seemed resigned to her daily medicine dose but her food continued to remain untouched. We tried to encourage her to eat by carefully forcing small amounts of food into her bill. If she swallowed even a morsel she might soon recognise the mash meant nourishment. By swishing our fingers in her water we even tried to imitate the dabbling noises a swan makes as it searches and sifts for food in the wild. Hope would regard us blankly. Our efforts meant nothing to her.

Then on her fifth day with us, to our relief, we saw the first faint indentation of a probing bill in her food bowl and her drinking water was clouded with chick crumbs. Hope had at last turned the tide. Her appetite returned and she grew from strength to strength. Under the vet's advice we removed the strapping from her wing to allow air to get at the wound and speed its healing. The enteritis responded to treatment and we no longer needed to dose her. She regained the use of her legs and within a week was so improved that she was allowed her first swim on the pond in the outside run. It was wonderful to see how she revelled in the feeling of water beneath her again, plunging and flapping and giving loud bugle calls as she washed away the dirt of her illness.

In Answer to the Cry

With such progress we anticipated a full recovery but as the days passed her injured wing began to droop badly at the tip. We put a strapping around it to give it support but when this was removed three weeks later the flight feathers immediately dropped again. Eventually we had to face the tragic fact that irreparable damage had been done to the tendons and muscles of the wing. Hope would never fly again.

It was doubly sad to realise that she had been maimed through human callousness. Ironic, too, that the powerful wings which had carried her so many thousands of miles from the far north should have made their last 'flight' silent and folded above the Cornish sea in a helicopter, a creation of man, born of his desire to emulate the freedom of the birds.

We now had to find a suitable and permanent home for our poor swan and so approaches were made to the Severn Wildfowl Trust at Slimbridge on the Severn Estuary in Gloucestershire. They kindly agreed to accept her. She was taken there by a friend and one of the staff and released among many companions in surroundings where she could remain content for the rest of her life.

The species of swan most frequently brought to the hospital is the Mute, familiar to all who visit the ponds, lakes and rivers of this country. In their wild life they have a reputation for being fierce and an ability to break men's legs or arms with their wings. In the confines of the hospital, however, it has so far been found that their aggressive hissing and neck-arching are a lot of bluff. In fact it is only their large size which presents us with a difficulty. Carrying a fully grown swan under one's arm takes a bit of doing. But once they are caught they almost collapse and give up with a few hisses of protest. They usually stick their neck straight out when being carried, and this can make negotiating doors and gateways somewhat difficult. On the whole they accept 'captivity' quite well and once they get the idea of eating their chick crumb mash out of a bowl have enormous appetites.

Newcomers to the Hospital

Peggy Bell now takes up the story as she had some amusing times with swans:

My first experience of handling one of these huge birds still makes me blush. He was oiled and brought to us by people who had found him in a creek near Fowey on the south coast of Cornwall. He had to have a dose of medicine to make sure he had no oil in his stomach. It was a large dose so it had to be administered by our holding open his beak and tipping some of the contents of a bottle down his long neck.

He was housed in a run with a pond. I was then given instructions by Olga, our warden. She told me to get behind the swan, and, as she caught hold of his neck, to stand astride his back and clamp his wings to his side with my knees. It worked like a charm; but as the medicine started to run down his neck he gave a terrific jerk and freed one wing. I held on for dear life, but I received a half-blow on my arm before I managed to clutch the wing with my hands, and by then the swan and myself were off balance and we fell in the pond of ice-cold water. I still held on to the swan and we thrashed around until Olga hauled me out.

He made a wonderful recovery and several weeks later his rescuers fetched him to be released near the spot where he had been found.

One summer afternoon the phone rang; it was a call from the Police Station at Hayle. A sick swan was out on the estuary and he had caused a traffic jam on the busy A30 road by coming off the mud-flats and limping to and fro across the highway. Could we come and collect him? When I arrived and asked for the swan, a police officer informed me, 'He is down on the mud-flats.' Apparently the long arm of the law hadn't been able to reach far enough to catch him.

Accompanied by the constable I went down to the water, armed with a sack and a piece of string. I waded out and caught up with the swan, but found it impossible to get his body into the sack. So staggering under the weight of the bird, which I had caught by getting his long neck under my arm and then clutching tight with both arms round his middle and with his large feet paddling in front of me, I made my slow way back to firm ground, my wellingtons sinking into stinking mud at each step. I looked up to find quite a crowd of people awaiting me. The policeman offered to hold the sack, after asking which was the dangerous end of the bird, and soon the swan was safe inside, with the sack tied neatly round his long neck. He was placed on the back seat of the car and hissing furiously was conveyed to the hospital. Fed and cared for, his injured foot healed, he was released one bright morning back to the wild and joined his 'family' in the waters of the estuary.

One September we were told that twenty swans were in trouble at Falmouth, the historic port nearly thirty miles away on the south coast, with plumage contaminated by oil. Some of the staff went over to investigate the report and found nine of the birds were only very slightly affected and could be dealt with on the spot. The other eleven were brought back to the hospital as they were in a bad condition. Their underparts were thickly tarred and the snowy plumage of their wings was stained where they had rubbed their long necks in an attempt to preen away the oil.

The prospect of cleaning eleven fully grown swans was somewhat daunting but, as the saying goes, where there's a will . . . and we certainly managed to find the way. The sea birds' big run was commandeered for the purpose and the ejected gulls took turns to peer in astonishment through the netting door of the main run at the 'pantomime' taking place.

One member of staff, clad from head to toe in oilskins as if expecting a force nine gale, sat on the sloping roof of the gulls' little shelter with a swan firmly held upon her lap. Its great expanse of oiled stomach was soaped and sponged clean by two more helpers. The swan's initial honks and hisses of protest were ignored, though its huge flapping feet sometimes sent the sponges flying across the run. In the end our patient conceded defeat and

Newcomers to the Hospital

draped its long neck around its captor's shoulders. Its head hung limply downward like a grotesque corsage, and with an expression of martyrdom it watched as oil and soap suds were rinsed away with buckets of warm water. One by one all the swans underwent their cleaning, though at the end of the performance it was a matter of debate as to who in fact was wettest, the staff or the swans.

Fortunately all survived their traumatic experience, birds and humans alike! When fully recovered the swans were transported in a convoy of vans back to the River Fal to rejoin the others.

A phone call of much more recent times brought us into contact with a swan of great character. He had been found by a lady living near Halamanning, a tiny village east of Marazion, some ten miles drive around the bay from Mousehole. Whilst walking around her small-holding that morning she had spotted the swan lying on a piece of waste ground. He had landed some yards short of a patch of marshland and a stream which feeds into the river Hayle. Beyond the marshes is a 'road' of ruined tin mine workings with broken chimney stacks and spoil heaps that stretch all the way to Camborne. It was a desolate spot, made even more inhospitable by the near gale force wind roaring in from the south-west. The swan was quite unable to walk, and his finder sensibly fixed a barricade around him to shelter him from the wind whilst he awaited the appearance of his 'ambulance'.

On his arrival at the hospital we unanimously agreed he was the largest swan we had ever seen – a truly magnificent bird. We should have been more inspired as to our choice of name for him, however, he was never referred to as anything but Swannee.

From the start he was something of a mystery. We had the feeling he was quite old and speculated that he might have lost his mate and become a solitary swan. Swans pair for life and never seek another partner. Whatever his past, we were sure that at some time he had been in close contact with humans. When the customary offerings of water and mash were given him, he instantly began to pick out mouthfuls of food and rinse them in his water bowl as if he had done this all his life.

We felt an immediate affection for Swannee and his infirmity caused us great concern. Whilst the right leg seemed perfectly normal, the left was very hot and swollen at the 'ankle' joint. He could not bear to put his weight on it to stand, let alone walk. But no break could be felt and, because of the solid thickening of the joint, we diagnosed a form of arthritis – an ailment compatible with his age. We rubbed the foot and joint with a soothing cream which had been recommended for leg troubles in oiled birds. It was over a week before he painfully hobbled the few steps from his house to the outside run where he sank on to the pond we had filled for him. The moment his legs no longer had to take the great burden of his weight he arched his neck and fluffed out his feathers, as if to say 'This is just what the doctor ordered!' We put his food by the edge of the pond and he spent all day floating and eating to his heart's content.

Swannee seemed to have so much faith in his water-therapy that we decided to put him in the run with the deep wide pond which would provide him with more swimming space. To our delight his leg began to respond to the hours spent swishing to and fro in the cool water. He was admired by the many summer visitors who start to climb the hill from the village and, finding our hospital sign two-thirds up, decide to discover what lies beyond the zig-zag flight of steps which leads to the sanctuary. Swannee presented a perfect picture of contentment in his sheltered pen amongst the trees and bushes, drifting on his pond with his stately image mirrored in the still water.

The only times that his dignity left him was on the occasions when we had to clean out his pond. Because of its size this is an undertaking of some length and it has to be completely emptied. Poor Swannee was so devoted to his water-therapy that he would just float there, gradually descending with the level of the water,

Newcomers to the Hospital

like a true captain going down with his ship. We used to find him standing pathetically on the concrete bottom unable to climb out of the steep sides. When we scrubbed and brushed around him he shuffled out of our way, hissing his disgust. Sometimes we would lift him out, but usually he stayed with us until, as the pond was re-filled, he could come up again on the 'rising tide'.

We watched with joy the steady improvement in his condition and began to think about his release. But where could we send him? Although he now walked with barely a limp, we had grave doubts about returning him to the wild. Swans can be extremely territorial and we felt younger and stronger birds might harry him unmercifully. Then one morning we received an out-of-the-blue phone call informing us of the death of one of an only pair of swans on a lake. It was the 'cob' who had died and we were told that his bereaved mate seemed very lonely without him. Though we had some reservations about her reception of Swannee we decided to accept the offer of a new home for him at Tehidy. After all, if things did not work out, we could always bring him back to Mousehole.

The secluded lake lay in the extensive grounds of a hospital. Fringed with trees, reeds and giant bullrushes it seemed everything a self-respecting swan could wish for. Swannee arrived there on a date pre-arranged with the head gardener, after being transferred to a Land Rover which was the only vehicle capable of making the drive through the woods. With some trepidation, he was released from his travelling basket and he moved out on to the lake. At the opposite end the resident swan spotted him and bore down on him like a ship in full sail, neck curved and wings arched in aggression. The worst was feared. Yet, as the two birds met, the pen's feathers sank sleekly back into place. All suspicion faded and she led Swannee away on a conducted tour of his new home.

Some weeks later we had to take a young mallard over to a friend at Praa Sands. His stretch of river has become a 'clearing house' for our orphaned ducklings when they are old enough to leave us. In

In Answer to the Cry

his office was a photograph of a beautiful swan. When questioned about it, he told us that the swan had been one of a pair brought to him from Hayle estuary some months ago. They were very old, well over thirty, and the lady who had fed and watched over them for many years became concerned for their safety when a new, stronger pair had started to encroach upon the pensioners' territory. Our friend remarked that the cob was the largest swan he had ever seen and that he and his mate had stayed with him for several weeks. Then, all of a sudden, they had taken off together and never returned.

With growing excitement dates were compared. Swannee had come into our care not long after the pair had vanished and Halamanning was on a direct flight path from Praa Sands to Hayle. These facts and his acceptance of captivity, his instant recognition of a feeding bowl, his age and above all his huge size seemed too much of a coincidence. We were convinced he was one of a pair and that as he and his mate had been heading for home, some unknown disaster had separated them and brought him into our care.

*

Beside the patients described in the girls' records above, mention must be made of the other unusual birds that came to the sanctuary over the years. Amongst them were a bittern, shelduck, horned grebe, a velvet scoter, tufted duck, black-tailed godwit, hoopoe, Bewick swan, little stint, wheatear, reed warbler, spotted flycatcher, tree creeper, eider duck, and a brambling, a bird not often seen here.

The number of birds brought to the hospital during 1966 was the highest ever recorded up to then, with 1,865 admissions. This number of admissions has only once been exceeded and that was in the following year when the terrible *Torrey Canyon* disaster occurred.

VIII
The Dark Shadow Falls

Life went busily on for the hospital during the sixties and all was going well. Then, on 18th March 1967 the great shock came. On the radio early morning news we heard that the giant oil tanker, the *Torrey Canyon*, had struck the Seven Stones Reef just north-west of the Scilly Islands, fifteen miles west of Land's End and barely twenty-five miles from us here, and the oil was discharging in vast quantities into the sea. We knew what this terrible news would mean for our sanctuary. The staff at once worked desperately hard to finish all the routine work so as to be ready.

Pog and I got the studio prepared to take in oiled birds by getting the fire going, the water heater on and making comfortable dark corners where the birds could rest and recover a little from the awful experience they would have been through.

This is Pam's account of all that happened on the dreadful days that followed, something none of us will ever forget.

Friday, 14th March 1967. The papers called it Black Friday, the day of the Black Tide and the Black Death. The dramatic headlines were well-earned for it was the day the oil from the huge wrecked tanker *Torrey Canyon* first came to the Cornish beaches and, for us at the RSPCA Wild Birds' hospital in Mousehole, it was the day Operation Bird Wash began.

In Answer to the Cry

Ever since the morning when the *Torrey Canyon* had run aground on the Seven Stones Reef we had been expecting an influx of oiled birds. None had come. The prevailing winds had kept the oil – and the birds – out at sea. There was plenty of evidence that the oil was affecting bird life, both from the reports of the local fishermen and the number of herring gulls about, whose grey and white plumage was spattered a dirty brown.

The only oiled birds we had as patients were ones that had been brought to us earlier in the year but they had already been cleaned and were well on the way to be fit for release.

The night before Black Friday I was on late duty at the bird hospital. Looking down on the houses below I noticed that the smoke from the chimneys was blowing towards St Michael's Mount and Marazion in the inner curve of the bay. The wind had changed. I remember thinking to myself, 'This is it. This'll bring in the oil', and feeling a sharp pang of anticipation.

As dusk fell I saw disturbances in the sea beyond the rocky shore below. Black specks were coming in across the waves, some thrashing the water like torpedoes, others drifting in with the rising tide. They were the first *Torrey Canyon* birds I saw, desperately beating their way to safety before the advancing oil.

The next morning Mount's Bay was unnaturally glassy smooth. A lonely naval vessel was spraying a narrow channel on to a slick of oil that a flotilla couldn't have cleared.

At the Bird Hospital all was normal. We decided to do our routine work as quickly as possible, knowing that it was only a matter of time before the first oil victims would arrive. We had over two hundred other birds in our care. Their welfare was a full-time job in itself without the added complication of an oil emergency. Pigeon loft, aviaries and cages had to be scraped and scrubbed clean, those of jackdaws and crows twice a day as they are particularly messy birds. There were seagull runs to be brushed and hosed down and four stone of fish to be cut up for their occupants. Meals had to be prepared for the other birds.

The Dark Shadow Falls

Treatments and first-aid had to be carried out when necessary.

The first oiled birds began to come in mainly from local beaches and only in ones or twos. We put them in the Guillemot House, a concrete house and pen built two years before, specifically for the housing of oiled birds. Since their numbers were not too great we were quite hopeful. If we kept to a proper routine we would manage. 'Proper routine' was a luxury we weren't going to see much of in the coming weeks.

The first indication that the *Torrey Canyon* affair was going to be something out of the ordinary was that the phone began to ring . . . and ring . . . and ring!

The calls were mainly from people wanting to know what they could do to help; or, to tell us they had found an oiled bird, could we deal with it? If not, what should they do?

In answer to the first enquiry we advised them to go out to the nearest beach, if that was possible, and pick up any oiled birds they found. To the second we replied we would take all birds if their rescuers could get them to us. At that time we had no transport at the hospital and, whenever possible, relied upon the goodwill of members of the public to bring us the birds; otherwise, the local RSPCA Inspector was informed and went round collecting them.

By the afternoon the number of birds being admitted was rising. It was obvious we were going to have to work overtime to keep pace with them.

The main sufferers of pollution were, as always, guillemots and razorbills. The guillemots outnumbered the razorbills by about eight to one.

Guillemots stand just over $16\frac{1}{2}$ inches high and are larger than the razorbills. They also have longer and much more pointed bills, whereas those of the latter are broader and the upper mandible hooks over the lower at the tip.

In perfect plumage razorbills are dapper little birds, closely resembling mini-penguins. They have chocolate or black heads, necks, backs and wings. The underside of their wings and 'shirt

The hospital records for the *Torrey Canyon* disaster; showing part of the entries for Easter Saturday and Sunday.

MARCH 1967

26 SUNDAY ○ Easter Day   WEEK 13 · 85-280

SS1
A ~~SS0~~
   200 /—Guillemots
   29 /— Razorbills.
A ~~SS1~~ SS0

A ~~SS0~~ SS1 Red Throated Diver (died 27-3-67)

A ~~SS1~~ SS2 Great Northern Diver. (✓ 7-4-67)
A ~~SS2~~ SS3 Great Northern Diver (✓ 7-4-67)

D Puffin (odm 25-3-67)   D 186

(Oiled Seabirds)

oil from Torrey Canyon wreck

R   15 Razorbills } Taken by Is   ✓ 38
R   15 Guillemots } Mr ~~Burkett~~.   ✓ 113
                      Taunton
D = 78 Guillemots   Died   D 264
D   8 Razorbills   Died   D 272

fronts' are brilliant white. The texture of their feathers is sleek and beautifully adapted to the long periods spent in oceanic migration. Their wings are comparatively short, streamlined and tucked close to their sides. In the sea they are superb swimmers, on land they are rather comic. They walk on their toes, leaning slightly forward, looking very industrious.

The razorbills now in our care presented a vastly different picture. Save for their heads, they were completely covered in brown, treacly oil. It didn't lie only on the surface of their feathers. It had sunk right down to their skin. Some had been rescued from sandy beaches and the grains of sand had collected on the oil making a coating as rigid as concrete. The birds had started to preen the oil from their clogged feathers, and the insides of their beaks and throats, normally pale pink, were stained bright yellow.

It takes two people to clean one oiled bird. One to wash and the other to hold. You can't tell a wild bird it mustn't struggle and these birds had suffered enough indignities and misery already.

First getting enveloped and choked by the thick black oil then the battle to get to the shore; perhaps a hectic chase across rocks or beach from the well-meaning rescuer; the fright of being handled by humans for the first time and then being thrust into a box, perhaps alone, perhaps with others; the dark journey to the hospital to be emptied out into alien surroundings and, after a rest, to be picked up again and held firmly whilst washed.

For the first time in the bird's life water breaks through its wonderfully devised waterproof feathers and touches its skin. It wriggles and helplessly squirms as slippery as an eel. You say gentle things to calm it, commiserate with it in its plight. Of course, it can't understand. Its beak snaps at anything and everything within reach. The person holding the bird has to wear gloves. A peck from a guillemot can draw blood. The razorbill and puffin hang on to flesh with bulldog tenacity. Larger birds, shags, cormorants, divers and the mighty gannet have to have their bills taped. One stab from *them* could mean the loss of an eye.

The Dark Shadow Falls

With four of us on duty that made two cleaning teams. We couldn't have had more, in any case, as we only had two sinks to work at. One was in the Guillemot House, the other in the small hospital building.

We used a lanolin-based, waterless hand cleaner for the actual cleaning process. This was put straight on to the oil and worked into the feathers. Finger-tip massage was the most effective means to do this. After at least five to ten minutes massage, varying with the amount of oil on each bird, it was rinsed thoroughly. The oil, now broken down, flowed off and gradually the plumage reappeared. There was almost always some oil stain left on the feathers but it was not sufficient to harm the birds when they started preening themselves dry before the fan heaters.

As soon as one bird was put down to dry off another was picked up to be washed, but, generally, cleaning went more slowly than usual. The phone rang continually, more and more birds were admitted and then a new hindrance materialised . . . Reporters!

For the past week newspapermen and newsreel camera crews had been hovering like vultures to get pictures and stories. One camera team had even suggested that we go out on a trawler so that they could film us picking up birds from the sea. Now they didn't have to go to such drastic lengths. The birds were coming in to the hospital in ever-increasing numbers – but not sufficient for one representative of a Sunday newspaper who was dismayed there weren't enough birds to present the gruesome front-page feature his editor required.

In fact the press were to prove a particularly unpleasant thorn in our flesh throughout the *Torrey Canyon* affair. Since we were almost totally naive and had had no briefing from RSPCA Headquarters on how to deal with a large-scale invasion of the press, we soon found ourselves completely overwhelmed. Sometimes it seemed there were more reporters than there were oiled birds. At best they were mildly annoying, at worst they brought our work to a standstill.

In Answer to the Cry

It was only in the peace of the evening that we were really able to get down to the washing. This was to be the pattern over the peak of the disaster. Early morning and evening were the only times we could count on not having our work disrupted.

Saturday saw us at work, if not bright then early, at seven o'clock, getting through as many of our set duties as possible before the invasion of birds and people started afresh. We didn't have to wait long. At this Easter weekend there were plenty of volunteers to scour the beaches for oil victims. Soon the ship's bell, half-way up the hospital steps, was signalling the arrival of new admissions. At first these were kept separate from the birds left over from Friday that we hadn't had time to clean. But eventually their numbers were so great that, for space's sake, we were compelled to let the two lots mix.

On Friday nearly two hundred birds had come in. Saturday brought us over two hundred more. On Sunday the figure doubled alarmingly. By Tuesday over one and a half thousand birds had been brought into our care, but, by then, our conditions had changed radically.

Washing operations had overflowed into the spare bathroom at Olga's house in the road just below and two teams were working there. One team at the wash basin, the other at the bath. The shed adjoining the bathroom had been fixed up to house cleaned birds. But it was obvious that, with space so limited at the hospital, other cleaning stations would have to be set up.

Headquarters posted down reinforcements of inspectors and clinic staff from Plymouth and London. Our first impression of the seven inspectors that arrived at Mousehole was, 'God almighty, what have they sent us!' Paste grey faces aren't set off to their best advantage by black uniforms. One or two looked more like undertakers' clients than bird rescuers. But, to do them justice, they had been travelling all night.

As well as RSPCA staff the RAC acted as 'collectors' and brought many birds to the hospital, and there were the Marine

The Dark Shadow Falls

Commandos, back from duty in Aden and now faced with a different sort of crisis.

In addition to official aid we were overwhelmed with offers of help from members of the public. In general, local people provided the most regular assistance at our hospital. Some whom we'd never met before, set to and became 'washers-in-arms', working as hard as any of us. The battle cry was, 'I don't mind what I do so long as I can help'. And help they did — with the washing of birds, cutting up fish, hosing down the seagull runs, answering the phone and even installing extra sinks in the Guillemot House. There was the Penzance Playgoers Society who took consignments of birds to clean, and the Penzance Round Table who transported seventy cleaned birds to Slimbridge in Gloucestershire where they were to recuperate. To some people, who had helped in the past, we gave the cleaning stuff and they turned their own homes into washing centres.

Those who travelled down to help from farther afield must have been rather disillusioned by the reception they got when they arrived here. Whilst we appreciated their sentiments they often proved to be more of a hindrance than a help, mainly because space was so limited at the hospital. Also the majority came for only a short time and it wasn't really long enough for them to get used to the work. But there were exceptions. Some came for a couple of days and fitted in as though they'd worked with oiled birds all their lives. Before we had time to thank them properly they had disappeared as quietly as they had come and all we knew about them was their first name.

In fact, the response of people to the plight of these masses of birds so cruelly damaged was quite staggering. Letters and donations began to flood in, some from people who knew Cornwall, or had visited the Bird Hospital, but many, many more from those who just cared.

Letter opening time was reserved for the evening when most of the people had gone and we had time to catch our breath. We sat, like mini-Shylocks, totting up the cheques, postal orders and cash, much sent anonymously, and all greatly needed. On some nights there was over £300. We had never seen so much money in our lives and, yet, it hardly seemed like money at all. Many of the accompanying letters were very touching, particularly those from the elderly and children.

We also had a large overseas mail, mainly from America, where we were bigger news than the Vietnam war, but also from Canada, South Africa, Australia and other countries. £4,000 was received at the hospital over the next two or three months. But it was the episode of the rags which eclipsed all other expressions of public generosity.

Our supply of towels, for the superficial drying of the birds before they were put in front of the fan heaters, had soon become exhausted. A notice was hung on the hospital gate. 'Old towels and soft woolly rags needed for drying oiled birds.' The children of Mousehole leapt into action. They went on a door to door collection, bringing back as big an assortment of rags as Steptoe ever saw. A lot of what was given was useless for our purpose. One didn't know whether to laugh or cry as our office, cramped at the best of times, was soon knee-deep with everything from shoes to corsets. From this jumble we sorted out the towels and sheets which we could use.

As if this avalanche was not enough a photograph of our innocent little sign appeared in a daily newspaper. I'd heard of the power of the press before but never seen it in action. Parcel after parcel, van load after van load of rags began to arrive at the hospital. It was like Christmas gone mad. Our beleaguered premises could not stand the strain. A nearby garage was commandeered and here all further parcels went.

Before long the garage was filled from floor to ceiling with literally tons of rags. Opening and sorting out the parcels became a full-time job. Sometimes money was enclosed with the rags. Stamps from the parcels were saved and given to charity. The rags we couldn't use were retained and these were eventually sold in bulk to a rag and bone merchant and so the donors' efforts were not wasted, for the money raised was added to the oiled birds' fund. In the end we had to put out appeals on radio and television, begging people not to send us any more. We were also given foam rubber sheeting, a huge box full of sponges, linen bags, cardboard pet carriers and scores of cardboard boxes.

And what of the birds, the unwitting cause of all this upheaval? By far the worst sufferers were the guillemots and razorbills but they were not the only species affected. There were shags and cormorants, both inquisitive-natured birds. They seem harder to clean than other varieties of diving birds. Their feathers are sleeker, tighter in texture. After cleaning they flip-flopped about on too large feet, slender necks snaking, beaks poking into everything.

The quaint, colourfully beaked puffins needed extra special care. Their sad, clown eyes seemed to express the misery of their plight. We had in too red-throated divers and their larger relative, the elegant great northerns, of the ruby eyes and spectacular black and white speckled plumage. They are shaped somewhat like a large goose and their legs and feet are so adapted to swimming that, on land, they can only move in ungainly frog-like leaps. Fear can make them extremely vicious and their method of attack is to leap straight up at one's face, a somewhat unnerving experience. They have a call quite unlike any other bird's. In the evenings the air would throb to their uncanny, sobbing cries. A number of gannets came our way too. These are magnificent, imperious birds with ice-blue eyes. They have a wing span of over 6 feet and their adult plumage shades from soft cream about the head and neck to pure white over the rest of the body, save for their flight feathers which are black. Immature gannets have a dark, speckled plumage.

Swans also managed to get themselves caught in the oil. But as has been told they are much easier to handle than one would imagine. They hiss fiercely and ruffle their feathers impressively but, once held, fold up and offer no resistance other than the occasional honk.

At first so many birds survived washing that we were faced with the problem of accommodating them. Soon we were full to overflowing and it was decided that suitable recuperation homes would have to be found. So, most of our cleaned birds had to be sent off to be cared for at Taunton, Bristol, Slimbridge and other places.

It is the after-care of oiled birds which is so difficult. The washing inevitably removes the natural waterproofing of their feathers. It takes a healthy bird six to eight weeks to recover this necessary oil and in captivity it becomes prone to disease. Post mortems revealed an astonishing list of ailments; peritonitis, enteritis, paralysis, nephritis, haemorrhage, aspergilliosis – a fungoid infection of the lungs – and avian tuberculosis and pneumonia. It is also believed that the after-effects of being oiled can cause brain damage.

Feeding these sea birds also presented a problem. The staple diet of ours was sprats, which were not always plentiful, but mackerel, filleted and cut into thin strips, also sufficed. They also required a vitamin additive to supplement their diet.

Towards the end of the first week of the *Torrey Canyon* disaster the number of birds being admitted was on the wane. By mid-day of Saturday, 1st April, there remained only three birds to be cleaned. A few hours later there were *three hundred and three*. It was a poor sort of April Fool!

The second influx of birds were in a far worse condition than the ones previously admitted. The oil had been on them just that bit longer. They were thinner and weaker. Many had swum the gauntlet of the oil only to be further injured by the detergents sprayed on the beaches. Their feet and beaks were badly blistered, something we had never encountered before.

Inevitably there came the time when the decision had to be

Right: The *Torrey Canyon* disaster, 1967 – a desperate and badly damaged gannet.

Below: Guillemots, other tragic victims of the oil spill.

Puffin, 'Tom Thumb', nearly ready for release.

A chance encounter.

Oil victim – a guillemot, fairly lightly oiled, but its eye shows little hope of survival for this bird.

Oiled guillemot is handed to Peggy Bell.

'Is there hope?'

Great northern diver with an injured leg.

Maggie, the magpie.

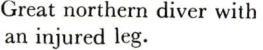

Baby gulls.

The Dark Shadow Falls

taken as to whether it was right to wash some of the victims at all. They were so obviously distressed or too much damaged that the kindest thing to do was to put them out of their misery. With some, their suffering was truly appalling. Without warning they would go into convulsions, literally screaming in agony. There could be only one answer to that. We destroyed them humanely, using an injection. Death was almost instantaneous.

In the mornings we always found a number had died during the night. We put the bodies in sacks, and later these would be collected and disposed of. Perhaps one of my most haunting memories was when these sacks were dragged down the hospital steps – they were too heavy to be carried. As they bumped from step to step the thought of all this suffering ending in death was quite overwhelming.

Olga tells of something that happened during these sad days which lightened the darkness. She heard the hospital bell ring, as it rings for every patient brought in, and saw a man standing there holding a large cardboard box. Hardly looking at him she went to take what she naturally thought was yet another oiled victim. He gave it to her, just saying, 'I thought you'd like something different for a change', turned away and went off down the steps. Olga took the box carefully up to the office, called one of us to come and stand by not knowing *what* might try and leap out of it. We opened the box, inside was a bit of paper on top on which was written: 'From Derek Tangye', and beneath we beheld a glowing mass of golden daffodils! What a blaze of hope and sunshine! We were much moved, as well as grateful, for the kind thought which had inspired Derek Tangye, the author, to help us like this. He lives a few miles along the coast and he and his wife have brought many birds to the hospital in the past.

The mental effect of working long hours – we started at seven each morning and except for meal breaks continued till ten at night – was positively numbing. The trouble was, there seemed no end in sight. Strangely enough, it was the return to what, at any other time, would have been routine work, that kept us from being completely overwhelmed.

It was sheer luxury to lose oneself up in the pigeon loft, or out in one of the aviaries, away from the hubbub of oiled birds, reporters, and countless other things. To treat a bird which wasn't oiled was a rare pleasure.

One such bird was a tawny owl found in a bad way at the side of a road. It didn't appear to be injured in any way but it was very dazed. We left it in a basket by the fire overnight. In the morning we discovered what had been ailing our unusual patient. In a corner of the basket was a broken egg. Our owl had been pregnant! She seemed a lot livelier, continued to make good progress and was later released back to the wild.

Then, slowly but surely, a semblance of normality began to return to our days. The number of oil disaster birds admitted dwindled and, this time, there were no relapses. Suddenly we weren't 'news' any more and the plague of reporters vanished almost overnight. We were able to tell our wonderful helpers we could cope without them and, at long last, we took proper time off work, something we hadn't done for nearly a month.

Soon all that was left of the *Torrey Canyon* affair was a garageful of rags, a vast number of sponges, a hoard of cardboard boxes, a year's supply of biological washing powder; towels and sheeting we are using to this day and . . . forty guillemots.

Through the crisis great interest in the birds' recovery had been aroused. We received several preparations which, it was hoped, would prevent disease and hasten their recovery. Some of the medicines were useful in the treatment of internal disorders but as so often in such cases time was shown to be the greatest healer.

A bird that has been cleaned from oil cannot be released until it passes its 'physical'. It must be completely waterproof – that is, even after prolonged swimming, water should roll off its feathers in droplets, never soaking into them. It must be 'on its toes' with no weakness in legs or feet. It must be well-covered with flesh. A

The Dark Shadow Falls

good indication of the fitness of a bird is to hold it in your hands with its wings free. The beat of the wings should be rapid and strong. In fact, if they strike your arms the effect should be so bruising that you have to put the bird down. The insides of the mouth must be pale pink and completely free of any tell-tale yellow oil stain. Its droppings must be pure white and liquid with no 'grittiness', mucus, or traces of blood.

To release a bird which does not comply with this 'standard' would be as sure a way of killing it as 'banging it on the head' as someone suggested should be done to *all* oiled birds.

We re-introduced our convalescents to water in careful stages. So long as the bird is strong enough the day after a washing to remove the oil, it is given a rinse in warm water (two-gallon buckets usually), repeated every subsequent day, until it is considered fit enough to be moved to the Guillemot House. Here it has free access to a shallow pool. Heat is always provided by a fan heater to help the bird dry off after cleaning. Later it is transferred to the deeper pond where it can splash, duck and dive to its heart's content.

On a glorious summer's day, appropriately enough 4th July, Independence Day in America, we took our first seven guillemots fit for release to Penberth Cove a few miles away. Let out of their boxes, they stood on the rocks for a minute or two, fluffing up their feathers in the warmth of the sun. Then they were gone, bobbing and diving their way to freedom. We were to make two more similar trips before the year was out.

The following April we received back from Taunton twenty-six guillemots, the survivors of those we had sent to them at the height of the crisis. After rest and testing out at the hospital these twenty-six were released successfully.

Four thousand birds had been cared for here, and with those dispersed to other centres, and those found dead or dying, the disaster was responsible for eight thousand birds received at the hospital. Many, many more were helped by other people or washed up dead, all along the coast. Countless thousands too must have been lost at sea and never recorded.

There are no words with which to express the full horror of such a death and on such an enormous scale, in spite of all human efforts to alleviate the suffering. Many people said ours and others' efforts were wasted, that the birds should have been destroyed on the beaches, that only the fittest, most lightly oiled should have been washed. They may be right. But it is always easy to stand back and expound theories in retrospect.

When you are presented with a *living* creature, in need of help, your natural instinct is to see what can be done to preserve that life. Dealing death is so easy, a hard blow on the head, the hypodermic needle, it's done, over, in a matter of seconds. Of course, there are occasions when one does not hesitate to free a bird from its suffering but there are others when you feel you've got to give it a chance. And, there is another thing. The oil hazard to birds is not a natural one. It has been created by man and so, perhaps, we feel that bit more guilty and a desire to make amends.

Visitors to the Bird Hospital often say, 'It must have been terrible for you when the *Torrey Canyon* went down'. Nowadays to recall that time is like remembering a bad, far-distant dream. It is hard to believe that once over eight thousand birds passed through our hands. Eight thousand birds, fourteen different species; the equivalent of four years' total intake of birds crammed into one hectic month. The excitement, the flashlights, the whirr of cameras, the T.C. labels stuck on cars; the scientist who came with a theory the birds were dying from malaria; the conscience-stricken American, with shares in *Torrey Canyon*, who flew over to rescue oiled birds; the two clinic boys from London who got soaked to the skin retrieving small boys, not birds; the tall, rather gaunt Inspector who earned the nickname 'Rommel' from his habit of travelling in the back of a Land Rover with binoculars glued to his eyes; the moments of anger, frustration, disillusionment and humour; the stench of the birds and the oil, these and other

The Dark Shadow Falls

jumbled memories are all that remain of that horrifying time for us.

Yet, oil pollution neither began nor finished with the *Torrey Canyon*. It had started in the years before and continues with us still; between the months of January and April, when the majority of diving birds are on migration, the ship's bell at the Bird Hospital has rung out to announce the arrival of many oiled birds. Even without an exceptional disaster we expect to treat at least two hundred. Next year it will be just the same.

*

After reading Pam's account one feels the numbers saved from the tragedy were indeed pitiful; but also it must be remembered that in nature's catastrophes of earthquake, tidal wave or avalanche the end is the same — some thousand human beings may die and few survive. Those who do must have songs of gratitude in their hearts for the miracle of life. Maybe the birds too have a feeling of joy in *their* hearts as they return to a life of freedom.

There is little more one can say about the disaster than has been said above, except to record that one good result followed. This was the contact made by the warden and staff with Newcastle University, where after the *Torrey Canyon*, exhaustive studies were made into oil pollution as it affected the birds. This came about through a visit to the sanctuary made by the late Dr Gregory of the University. Problems of oiled birds were discussed in detail. Another useful visit was paid by Mr A Taylor, also from Newcastle, who was working there, with Professor Clark, on their investigations.

The method advised by them resulted in notable success as long as the polluted birds were found and brought to the hospital quickly for treatment. If the rescue was delayed and the oil absorbed internally by preening, and the bird in poor condition, the result was disappointing even though the Newcastle method of cleaning had been used.

In Answer to the Cry

A very helpful gift that came during the crisis was that of several sink water heaters from the director of the firm that made them. He very kindly had them adjusted to the right heat necessary for rinsing the oiled birds. His interest was so real that he rang up every evening to ask how things were going and how many new birds had come in.

Amongst the many hundreds of sympathetic visitors we had at this time was Mr J H Kirby, Chairman of the Board of Shell Tankers. He was deeply concerned at the sad plight of the birds, and said his company had spent much money on arrangements to prevent the cleaning of tanks at sea, which causes so much of the harm done to the birds.

Another visit we remember with pleasure was from Lord Greenwood, then the Hon Antony Greenwood, who was down on official business but kindly spared time to come and see us all. He was most interested in the work being done and thanked us all, finally giving me a lovely grip of the hand and saying, 'I am with you all the way'. A kind of benediction – no officialdom there.

A letter that came from America at this time was from Mrs Mallering, wife of one of the first 'Lone Sailors' to sail round the world. She wrote from America telling how when her husband was returning from his voyage she went to Falmouth where he finished his adventure. They then sailed on together to Penzance, and as they came into the Bay she remembered seeing our birds' sanctuary standing high on the Mousehole hillside. In her letter she told of the happy memories of that time which were awakened by her reading in the newspaper about the tragedy of the *Torrey Canyon*. She was sad to think of all the suffering that would follow for the birds and sent a very kind donation to help with the extra work she knew would now have to be done here.

Many of our personal friends sent gifts for us to spend as we thought best to help the oiled birds. Always we had wanted a really deep pond where the divers could finally be tested out before release. So we planned to have one made at the end of our garden,

The Dark Shadow Falls

adjoining the Bird Hospital, with suitable shelters and large rocks on which they could perch as they spread their wings, after their dives in the pond, in preparation for the real flight to come.

A board by the entrance reads:

> Given in Memory
> of the Birds
> who lost their lives
> in the
> Torrey Canyon Disaster
> March, 1967

IX
The Torrey Canyon

It was not until some weeks after the great tanker had struck the rocks that we heard all the details of the terrible event. It is described here by one of our old friends, who belongs to this part of the world and is a devoted student of birds. In outline this is what happened.

In the middle days of March 1967 the *Torrey Canyon*, one of the largest ships in the world, was steaming up towards the Scilly Isles from the Cape. Nearly 1,000 feet long, and with a beam of 125 feet, she was carrying 120,000 tons of crude oil from the Persian Gulf to the refinery at Milford Haven on the south-west coast of Wales. She followed this longer route around the Cape because with that weight aboard she was much too deep in the water to go through the Suez Canal.

The date of her approach is important for at this time of the year large numbers of sea birds are also coming up from the south along their old migration route, to mingle and rest for a while with the local island birds before continuing their flight towards their breeding grounds further north. This year some thousands of those birds, alas, would never reach their destination.

The coastal route between the English and the Bristol channels passes fairly close to Land's End, keeping well to the east of the Scillies. Ships coming up from the south and heading for ports on the west side of Great Britain steer a course west of the Bishop

The Torrey Canyon

Rock lighthouse and the islands. This presumably was the route the *Torrey Canyon* was following. But the ocean currents are unpredictable in this part of the Atlantic with a trend towards the east and frequent bearings have to be taken. In the course of a full day's run, unless careful corrections are made, they can move a ship off course by as much as twenty or thirty miles. The *Torrey Canyon* must have neglected this possibility of error, for on the early morning of 18th March when she came in sight of the Bishop Rock in the south-west area of the Scillies, she was considerably east of her designed course and heading north-east. To avoid the islands she had to alter course; either westwards, to round them on the outer, oceanic side; or more to the east, in order to pass through the dozen miles of navigable channel between the Scillies and Land's End. The former course would have taken roughly half an hour more than the latter. The chief officer was on the bridge at the time and he changed course northwards towards the Bishop Rock, with the intention soon afterwards of going still further west around the outer islands. But the captain joined him then and on ascertaining that her former course would take the ship clear of the islands on the east side, he changed her back to that direction once more. He had to get to Milford Haven as soon as possible. He knew that if he missed the evening tide there the ship would have to wait several days before she could dock because of her exceptional draught. If he went around the islands he would lose that extra half hour! Just half an hour! It was a decision which, extraordinary and irresponsible in itself, involved other possibilities of danger which should have deterred him. It is always dangerous when a ship of that size comes in too close to the land, and the coastal waters now just ahead of him had special dangers of their own. Already they could see some local fishing boats ahead, with buoys here and there marking their fishing nets, and the ship was going at full speed, seventeen knots, and was still on automatic steering which allows a change of course of only three degrees at a time.

The *Torrey Canyon*, having rounded St Mary's and the Eastern

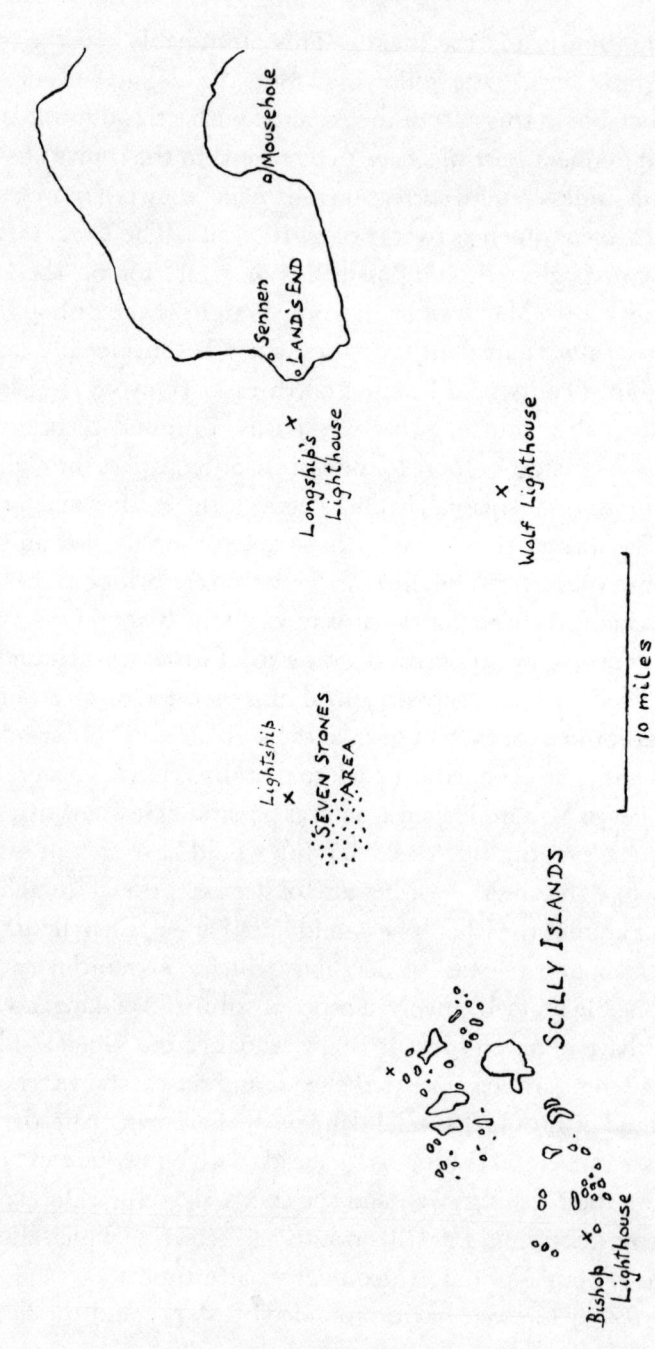

The Torrey Canyon

Isles, was soon approaching the area of the Seven Stones to the north-east, so called because at low tide seven rocks are visible standing some feet above the water. This area was probably once an island of some size, submerged to no great depth now by a drop in the level of the land that occurred subsequently to the one that separated the Scillies from the mainland. Because of its danger to shipping there has been a lightship there for over a hundred years. It is off the regular trade routes however and ships of any real size have no reason to pass near.

The captain now made another surprising decision. Instead of passing the Seven Stones to the east and entering the broad and safe strait between them and the mainland at Land's End, he decided to alter course to port, presumably once more to save a little time, so as to pass through the narrow and more dangerous channel between the Seven Stones and the islands. But a fishing boat on their port side prevented that turn for a time, and when they were less than three miles from the nearest of the Stones another fishing boat prevented a second and even more vital turn. The utter madness of what was happening seems incredible to us now. This was not one of those dreams we have in which danger is approaching and we are helpless and cannot somehow get out of the way. This was in the broad light of day, with the weather and visibility good. It was tempting providence, courting danger. He had 120,000 tons of crude oil in his hold, he was still going at full speed, and to add to the danger the tide had been ebbing for nearly two hours! Even then it was not too late however. He could still by changing course to starboard have rounded the Seven Stones on the safe, east side. But he didn't. Even when he decided belatedly to change from 'automatic' steering to 'hand', some time was lost because of a misunderstanding with the switch involved. He was still going at full speed when with warning rockets being fired from the lightship they struck a submerged ridge on the western side of the Pollard Rock, the largest of the Seven Stones. When she struck the captain ordered full steam astern, but as one of the crew

In Answer to the Cry

said afterwards the sea following on in the great ship's wake 'pushed her further on'. There was a loud grinding and crashing along the length of her keel and the first stream of those 120,000 tons of oil was pouring out into the sea.

When the little SS *The Scillonian* takes you on the delightful sea-crossing from Penzance to St Mary's Island in the Scillies, past our little fishing village of Mousehole where the bird hospital looks down upon the harbour and St Clement's Island just outside, with the mainland receding then from view astern and the low configuration of the islands becoming clear ahead, every now and then you disturb little groups of sea birds, guillemots, razorbills, puffins, shearwaters and other species, resting on the water or flying to and fro across the bows, like a little home fleet of birds. See with what zest and vigour they skim away across the freshly lapping wavelets, half running and half flying, as we too in our forward movement are filled and uplifted with the abounding freshness and the age-old purity of the sea. They are small in number here in mid-passage compared with those we shall see on the islands if our object in going there is to seek out the birds.

The Scillies are surely among the most attractive of all the island groups of the world, especially among those, where by their very nature, sea birds are much older and much more numerous colonists than man. The best known of them are St Mary's, the largest, but only about $1\frac{1}{2}$ miles across and $2\frac{1}{2}$ miles long; then St Martin's, and Tresco with its tropical vegetation and its Valhalla of the figure-heads of ships wrecked on the island shores; and smaller still, Bryher, St Agnes, Samson and Annet. In addition to these are a host of smaller islands and bare rocks that crowd, above and below the surface, all around them, as if scattered there by nature's own hand. The whole group is surrounded, especially one feels on the western side, by the great range and hidden power of the Atlantic, invaded always by the driving freshness, the dash and splash and breaking of its waves.

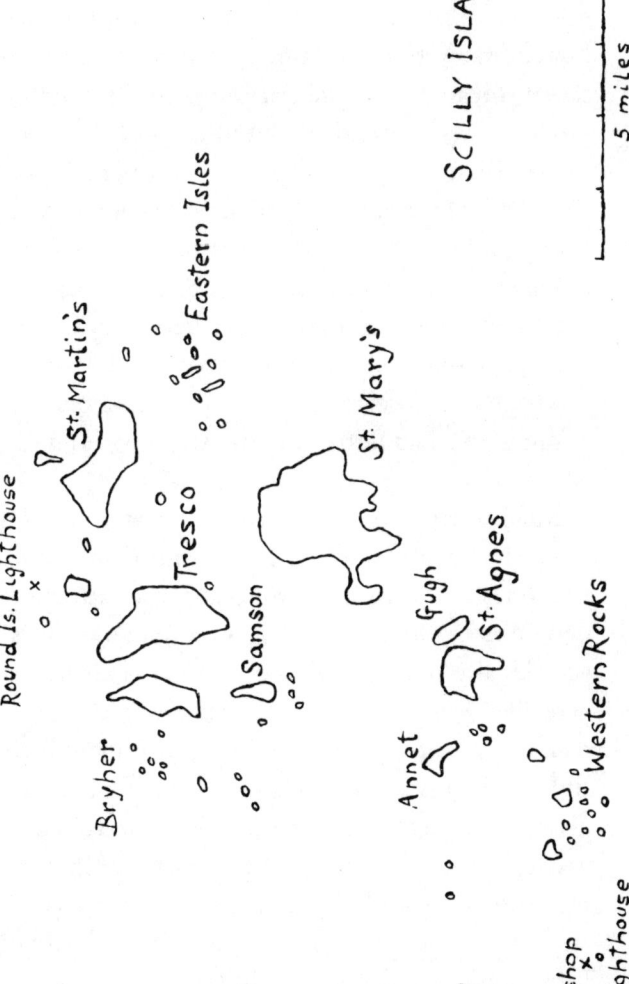

In Answer to the Cry

When *The Scillonian* lands you at Hugh Town in St Mary's, you have a choice of local trips in almost any direction. If you have been a frequent visitor, you will go perhaps down beyond Annet to the Western Rocks, or northwards to the Eastern Isles, between St Mary's and St Martin's, in a longitude slightly more to the east than they. On a calm day you are safe enough in a small and easily handled boat there, changing direction slowly over the changing contours of the sea floor. Too small, even the largest of them, for human habitation, the birds have them to themselves. You will see, if you are lucky, the charming puffin standing on a rock, with half a dozen tiny fish hanging loosely from the grip of its extraordinary bill. Clever little fisherman! God bless and protect him. But who would wish to harm or molest him or put an end to his joy in life and his peaceful trade, in his chosen domain. Other members of the auk family will be there, and at a different time you might even surprise the lovely kingfisher, working alone perhaps in some solitary place, on one of its own 'halcyon' days, its plumage deep ocean-blue and white and orange-brown, diving, rising with a fish in its bill, and slapping it on the granite rock on which it stands.

Much further to the north of the Eastern Isles, through your binoculars you will see the lightship marking the Seven Stones, where the currents are strong and the fathoms change abruptly underneath, a region rarely visited, though an islander no doubt occasionally sets foot on one or more of them at low tide. It was here the *Torrey Canyon* struck. There is a tragic irony in the fact that nature throughout the years has endowed the birds with oil and oil glands of their own to keep their bodies in condition, giving and preserving for them that marvellous and unrestricted freedom of the air, and that now they and that exquisite plumage are being destroyed by the crude oil that man in the pursuit of his own ends carries so dangerously across the oceans of the world. The *Torrey Canyon* disaster brought the tragedy closer home to us, but for years before birds were being killed by the deliberate practice of jettisoning waste oil when ships wash and clear out their tanks at sea.

The *Torrey Canyon* grounded on the Seven Stones at about nine o'clock on the Saturday morning of 18th March, and the powerful tug *Utrecht*, a familiar sight at anchor in Mount's Bay which she uses as a base for her salvage operations, set off at full speed and was alongside the wreck by 11 a.m., thus securing for her company the salvage contract. One or two other craft in the vicinity followed; the Scilly and Mousehole lifeboats were also quickly there, and two helicopters came across from the naval air station at Culdrose on the Lizard peninsula. As the magnitude of the task of rescue became known three or four other tugs eventually arrived.

When the ship struck, the sea was calm and the weather clear; but soon afterwards the wind increased and visibility deteriorated. The water was too rough and too shallow for the *Utrecht* to get alongside and the Scilly lifeboat transferred the first salvage officers to the wreck. The plan at once was to pull her off the rocks at high tide that same evening, and the *Torrey Canyon* crew were already busy pumping out the oil into the sea to lighten the ship for that purpose. The sea could be polluted, but the ship must be saved, and there would be a handsome reward for the salvage company if they succeeded. But by evening the wind had strengthened still more and the oil tanker began to roll slightly, increasing the damage to her hull, with the oil pouring out and drifting away in increasing quantities. The attempt to pull her off was made soon after 9 p.m. and it failed. The ship was listing, the engine room was flooded, and there were signs of a crack developing right across her hull underneath, just abaft of midships. It was soon realised that it was the fore part of the *Torrey Canyon* that was most firmly caught on the rocks, and the mad idea was at one time entertained of sparking off a series of explosions along that line of weakness in order to split the ship in two in the hope it would be possible to float off the stern half then and tow it

In Answer to the Cry

away! Tow it, if you please, up through the English channel, the busiest trade route in the world, to Amsterdam and thus save a good proportion of the oil — if it hadn't already discharged itself into the sea along its way!

In the days that followed three or four other attempts to shift her were made. Weather permitting there seemed a fair prospect of success, for the height of high tide was increasing and would continue to do so by as much as a foot a day until a week later when it would reach its peak of over twenty feet, on Monday, 27th March. More intensive preparatory work was done on the ship itself. Oil was still being pumped out all the time, and compressors were pumping in air to increase her buoyancy, and the pressurisation in the upper area of her tanks had also the effect of forcing more and more oil out through the holes and cracks below. This compressor work was dangerous, because a spark might ignite the gas that was rising thickly from the hold and there were several explosions caused by it. Preparations made to place a boom all round the ship for a concentrated spraying of the oil were never put into effect because of this same danger.

Most of the crew had been taken off the ship on the second day, and in the subsequent salvage work the officers and men needed were put aboard or taken off again as the weather improved or worsened. The attempts to pull her off were interrupted sometimes by gale-force winds. Waves, especially perhaps those out there around the Scilly Isles, will strike and pound relentlessly upon wrecks until they are destroyed, or until the surface sees them no more; and there were times now when they increased the escape of oil and contaminated the sea still more. For when the intense straining and dragging of the tug ropes widened the cracks and holes in the *Torrey Canyon* hull, the rocking action of the waves, each time they lifted up the port or the starboard side, opened further those cracks and holes and so greatly facilitated the outflow of oil.

All the attempts to get her off failed; and with each failure the

The Torrey Canyon

British Government was getting more and more worried by the widespread pollution of both sea and land. For ten days it had been going on and still the great ship was there, spilling out its oil. Bombing began on that tenth day and continued for several days after until the oil still in the ship had been destroyed. The problem facing the authorities had been a difficult one. How much escaping oil must be allowed to pollute the sea as long as there was still any real hope of salvage? Save the ship, or, to say nothing of other consequences, save the lives of many thousands of sea birds? In the event, they allowed 80,000 tons of crude oil to escape before our planes bombed and burnt up the 40,000 tons that remained. Surely they waited too long. In view of the reckless, irresponsible way the *Torrey Canyon* had been handled before she struck, I really do believe I would have sacrificed the whole of that ugly, ill-fated ship, oil and all, to save the life of just *one* bird.

Oil had started to come away from the *Torrey Canyon* as soon as she had struck; and there surely must be a fault in the structure of such a ship to allow such a thing to happen. Ships of the Royal Navy started their spraying operations around her almost at once. As the days passed and the pollution increased more Navy ships came and they were assisted by smaller local craft. Helicopters were surveying the slicks on the sea, some of them half a dozen miles across and three or four times as long. One of them, before it split up into smaller patches, was estimated to have almost 40,000 gallons of crude oil. The fears uppermost in most people's minds were the devastating effects these slicks would have when they reached our shores, fears that later were abundantly justified. The emulsifying detergent that at first had been in such short supply was soon arriving in huge quantities, both for immediate use by the Navy and for the Army that was getting ready to deal with the menace on land, installing detachments of troops, thousands in all, at different places along the Cornish coast.

At first the wind was driving the oil southwards between the

In Answer to the Cry

Scillies and the Wolf Rock lighthouse. Curiously enough, the islands themselves though closest to the danger were in the end the least to suffer as hardly any oil was washed ashore there. The direction of the moving slicks was determined by the changing direction of the wind. When it blew from the south-west it carried the oil up along the north coast of Cornwall as far as Hartland Point, infecting it and its holiday beaches all the way. In all the coastal waters local fishing boats were out spraying the oil.

When the wind changed and came from the western quarter the oil struck straight against Land's End and into Mount's Bay. In spite of the numbers of soldiers employed, assisted as they were by many volunteers, it was quite impossible for them to meet the danger everywhere. Often, too, when a particular beach had been sprayed and cleaned, a local movement of the tide brought a new influx of oil that smothered it again. Some areas were luckier than others because of the lie of the land and local variations in the wind and tides. Two places perhaps that suffered most were Sennen Cove by Land's End and Porthleven on the eastern side of Mount's Bay. The stench and slime and filth at such places were almost intolerable; but the smell was to be found much further afield, over most of Cornwall itself and from Dartmoor and other districts in Devonshire. When finally the wind came more from the north it drove the oil down to the Channel Islands and the coast of Brittany, infecting the oyster and mussel beds and some of the little bird islands there, and all the steps that had been taken to combat the menace in England were now initiated by the French government.

At Sennen near here in those first days one could hardly believe such black pollution could have come in from the sea. It was an incongruous, alien association of ideas the mind found it difficult to accept, for the sea had always been a purifying influence, a very symbol of purity and never of pollution in the past. The cause one then bitterly reflected was man, 'homo sapiens' indeed, polluting both sea and land.

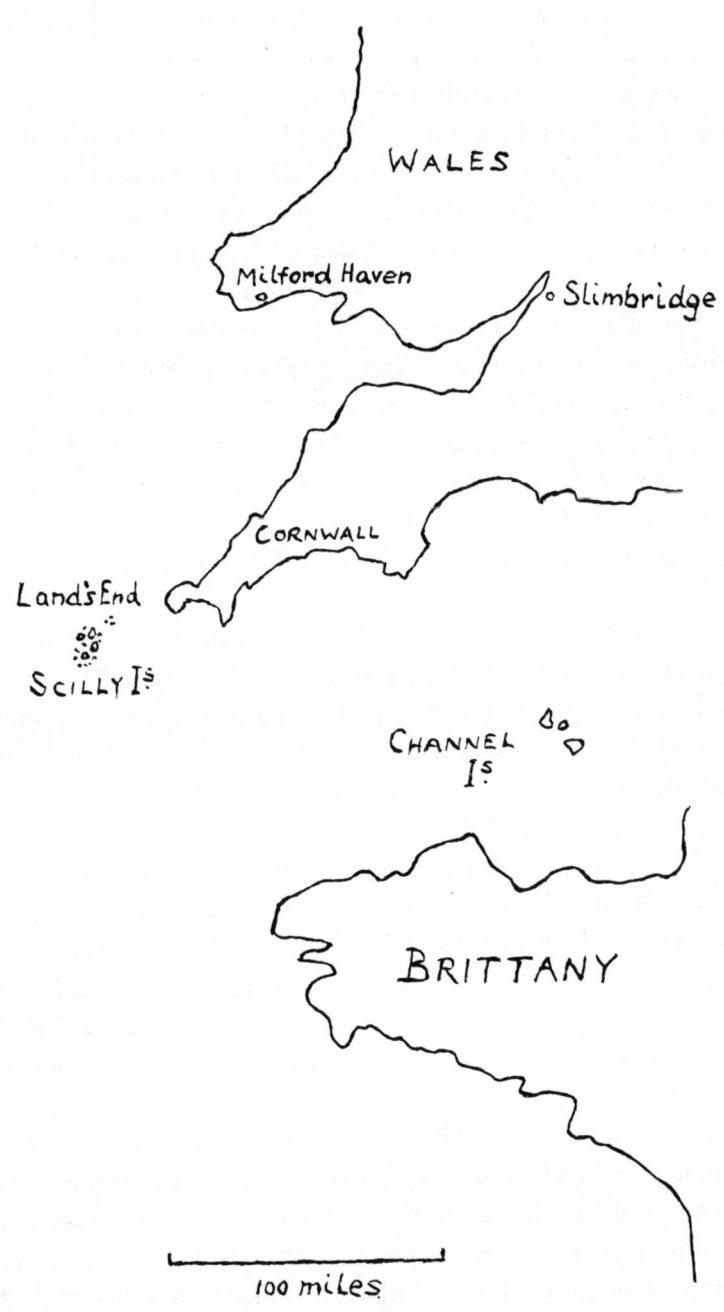

In Answer to the Cry

The 'battle of the beaches' attracted hundreds of spectators everywhere. Could the beaches be cleaned again in time for the visitors in the Easter holidays that were now near? There was some talk of the damage done to the marine life of the shore by the oil and the detergents used to remove it. The death of birds was mentioned from time to time but always rather in the background. It was 'the beaches' that had to be 'saved'. But to the naturalist and the nature lover the greatest tragedy in the whole of this *Torrey Canyon* affair was the shock and suffering and destruction it was causing to our sea birds. Exactly how many thousands of them perished we shall never know, least of all those lost and never recorded out at sea. But you could see them flopping and struggling in a host of places around our shores, trying to walk and extricate themselves from the coagulation of oil and sand, their plumage plastered with it, helpless, silent, bewildered, innocent and ignorant of the cause.

The preparation and organisation to deal with this sudden emergency were woefully inadequate and we should have been even less prepared if a few places like the Bird Hospital in Mousehole had not been there. One dreads to think of the future. Already there have been escapes of oil from platforms in the North Sea, and there is talk now of drilling for oil in the English Channel and the Celtic Sea. We pay for our sins in this world, especially for those committed against nature's laws. We have been pursuing our own selfish ends for too long. Pious hopes and prayers will not be enough. Man now, if only for the good of his own soul, must have regard to the sanctity of life in all forms, and must look at the problem for what it really is, a religious one in the widest sense of that word.

There is a poor lost guillemot down there, beneath that granite boulder, on the blackened sand; and as the filthy tide comes in and starts to wash its dead, unfeeling body to and fro, dead now to its own familiar world, it brings the pathos and our own sin and shame more closely home to us. The Ancient Mariner when he

The Torrey Canyon

killed the Albatross had its death upon his conscience for the rest of his days. What much greater load of guilt will rest upon the conscience of mankind if something drastic is not quickly done to eliminate this widespread danger before it gets even worse. As that unhappy mariner himself said:

> He prayeth best who loveth best
> All things both great and small,
> For the dear God, who loveth us,
> He made and loveth all.

X
The Birds Play their Part

The peace of mind, so essential to this work, yet sometimes so difficult to obtain, was indeed disrupted by the horror and tragedy of the *Torrey Canyon* and was only restored to Pog and me, who had been working virtually night and day with the oiled victims in our care, by our living contacts with the birds.

About this time a baby jackdaw was brought to the hospital and was called Billy after the boy who had rescued him just in time. He was uninjured but very young and bewildered. He settled in well with the other little ones and soon learnt to feed himself, his intelligence being of an unusual order even in those early days. When going on my 'rounds' at the hospital I always responded to his demand for something special. He took it readily from my hand, though he was beginning to be aware of the difference between those looking after him, whom he trusted, and visitors who were strangers to be avoided. This has always been the first sign to us that a bird is getting ready for safe release, and we released Billy soon afterwards. When our baby birds are fully grown, in perfect plumage, and obviously ready to go, the girls open the small release door and the little flock take off, some of them returning to sleep at night, then off again in the morning, till they start their independent existence.

One day, two or three months later I was up in the seagulls' run when I became aware of small feet pattering about on the wire-netting just over my head. I looked up, and there was that

The Birds Play their Part

face, unmistakably Billy, with the shining eyes and look of expectancy. Fortunately I always carry a 'cheese box', so was able to oblige with a bit of cheese. Having finished what I was doing I went back to Green Hedges, where we were living, and as I entered the door Billy suddenly landed on the window sill! He must have watched my movements very carefully to have timed it so well. Soon he was inside and on the back of my chair, looking very pleased with himself. After a good snack he was off again through the window. This happened every day but he would only come in if Pog and I were alone.

A year or two later we moved up to Love Lane Cottage which we had built on the land high above Green Hedges but still adjoining the sanctuary. Our only worry was lest Billy would think we had deserted him. We need not have worried. He evidently had taken note of our change of address, and on the second day, there he was, calling to pay his respects. He sat a minute on the window sill, inspecting, then, first flew on to the back of my chair and then on to Pog's, completely one of the family. After that every morning early he would come into my bedroom and help himself to a pan of food I had ready for him on the table beside my bed.

The following spring he was always in a frantic hurry, snatching up food and dashing off again. One morning I was reading in bed very early when I felt something land, light as a feather, on my knee. There was Billy, all excited, his feathers fluffed out, his expression one of bliss, the contentment of fulfilment. I got the message; a baby in the nest! Suddenly he calmed down and took off like a flash. How proud I felt at having been the first to be told the wonderful news. Each day he came, and then a few weeks later he was back into our sitting room again, calling to and answered by two beautiful young ones who landed simultaneously on the window sill. After that came the adventure of the window seat, and finally the strange floor to be discovered of the room inside. Pog and I sat still and silent leaving Billy in complete possession, while the babies yelled and flapped their wings until replete with the food their parent stuffed into their open mouths. Gradually their lessons were learnt, the food not put into their mouths but flung on the floor, where they were forced by hunger to feed themselves. Then they were taught good manners – to wipe their beaks on our unfortunate carpet. We could not help laughing at their clumsy efforts to copy the example set by the proud Billy but at last they got the idea. Result: two dapper, shining little birds and one grubby carpet. One of our very happy memories – and Billy continued to make this his second home for many years.

Another bird friendship we shall never forget was one with some starlings.

One spring day I was standing at the glass door leading from our room to the birds' balcony, when a mother starling flew in followed by three screaming young ones. She lined them up in a row on the long perch there, and then filled up their open mouths with the soft food I had just put out. When they were satisfied she flew off and they all followed instantly behind her, still making their shrill cries. They came each morning after that and took no notice of me, but I always kept the date as I loved watching them from the open door.

One day they came as usual, the babies yelling at the top of their voices, but Mother Starling ignored them, except to see that they lined up properly. Then she must have said something to them (unheard by me) because when she went off alone they with one accord turned round and flew at *me*, calling for breakfast with open mouths into which I hurriedly and clumsily stuffed food, as excited as they were. So I became Foster Mother, as definitely appointed by the real mother, a compliment I tried to live up to.

We called them The Poppies because all three were constantly popping up in the garden. We had most meals outdoors and there they were rushing about on our table, eating at first from our hands and gradually helping themselves. They appeared in the early mornings at our front door demanding cheese and life was entirely to their satisfaction.

The Birds Play their Part

That autumn we had a lot of rain. One day in a down-pour I heard them at the door and quickly gave them food. Two filled up and flew off but the third remained looking at me. He was soaking wet and then I saw that his right wing was hanging slightly from the shoulder. He could not fly and something had to be done. Fortunately a friend was with me, so we arranged that she should stand out of sight behind the open door, while I laid a trail of cheese from the doorstep to the kitchen which was nearby.

'Come on Poppy', I said, hardly daring to breathe.

Then he popped on to the doorstep, ate the cheese and followed the trail into the kitchen and on to a pail under the sink where he shook himself and proceeded to clean his feathers with absolute self-possession.

By this time the front door had been gently closed and a suitable packing case placed facing the kitchen door. Again I laid a trail of cheese into the cage, went very quietly into the kitchen and said, 'Go to bed, Poppy.'

He at once hopped off the pail and then straight into his house and up on to the bough where he continued his toilet.

We had the vet who said the wing was not broken, only strained and should recover in time. As it strengthened we put his house into the balcony each day, shutting the windows there and leaving the door of his house open. He would pop out flying more strongly every time.

At last the day came when we could open the balcony windows and let him go. He was in no hurry until a starling came and sat on the top of the open window. It too must have been one of the family Poppies because our Poppy at once joined the other and off they flew together.

After that he came back daily to the balcony and to the kitchen window. I knew him by the *very* slight droop still sometimes noticeable on his right wing which eventually folded back into its right place so that I could not tell him from the others who came. However he had already made a habit of arriving in silence but

In Answer to the Cry

always giving a shrill cry as he flew off. He never said 'Please' but *always* a 'Thank you', so I knew that all was well with him.

Another dearly loved bird was a male blackbird, brought to us at Love Lane Cottage by neighbours who thought he needed 'the intensive care unit', owing to his injuries. This bird had been fed by them at their kitchen window for quite three years. From the first visit they noticed one foot was missing, the leg itself being perfectly strong as was the other one. He had adopted their garden and built a nest there, coming regularly to their window for food. Then one day he apeared to have difficulty in landing on the sill and to their concern they saw his *good* foot was badly twisted. They managed to lure him inside, caught him, and brought him up to us. We all felt it looked a pretty hopeless job. He was so self-possessed however, settling down into the house we quickly prepared, instantly falling on the food, that we felt we *must* see if anything could be done.

The vet came, shook his head and said the break had already set. The ankle would have to be broken and *re-set*, and he felt the bird would not stand it and advised destruction. In the face of the bird's intense desire to live, as shown by his contented acceptance of his fate in our hands, we decided to put off the sad day for at least a little while. We gave him a soft bed of foam rubber in the corner of his house, which he took to at once, a lawn of short moss in which he could not catch his bad claw, a shallow bath and a pan of suitable food. We soon discovered his pet fancy was ripe pears. It became a kind of mania with him but they had to be Williams, home grown; all foreign pears he scorned.

In trying to think of a name for him we felt it should be something to do with pears but could think of nothing which would include that word except Peardrop, so that is what he became.

We put his house in a sunny window in my bedroom where he could see other blackbirds, thrushes, starlings and sparrows who came for their tit-bits to the kitchen window, near by. He seemed to like seeing them and never showed any signs of wanting to get out and join them.

One very early morning in the following March I was awakened just before dawn by a heavenly little 'murmuration' of song, so soft that I had to listen intently to be sure I was not dreaming. It was our little Peardrop making his first Ode to Spring. Each day it lasted a little longer and increased in volume. Throughout April it strengthened and he sang at short intervals during the day. Then on a glorious first of May he was in full song, beginning at a quarter to five in the morning and going on without ceasing for nearly an hour. From that day this joyous sound lasted from dawn until dusk. This background of music in our lives was with us until the longest day of the year, 21st June. Then he ceased his early morning greeting to the sun and only sang with longer intervals of silence till evening. By the middle of July the song had ceased, with a few murmurations sometimes until the end of November and then silence till March came round again.

This pattern was followed all the five years he was with us. When he was in full song, I would ring up friends in London or elsewhere, tell them to listen, and Peardrop's voice would soar above the noise and turmoil of the town bringing ecstasy to those who listened.

In the last year of his life, when he must have been about eight years old, murmurations started in January at dawn, but by March there were no more songs, only sometimes a tiny twitter when I said 'good-night' to him. But he was just as lively as ever, enjoying his food, especially the pear, and sleeping soundly at night.

Then, one evening, he had tucked himself up in his bed as usual and I was reading rather late, when towards midnight I heard a flap of his wings. I got out of bed and found he had moved on to the moss, but was perfectly quiet, so I left him undisturbed. A quarter of an hour later there was another single movement of his wings, and when I went to him he was lying quite still, with wings outspread and head resting on the moss. Our Peardrop had made

In Answer to the Cry

his last flight. He left a great blank in our lives. Somehow we knew it had been right to recognise his own great desire to live and so fulfil his destiny.

XI
The Bell Still Rings

The beautiful ship's bell which hangs halfway up the steps to the hospital, and which is rung by all those who bring patients to us, is inscribed with the words:

Neil Jager 1938-1951

The bell was given by his parents and friends as a memorial to this young boy, who greatly loved birds, and who had died in a tragic accident at the age of thirteen.

Pog and I, who had met the family earlier, felt at the time that the bell would ring through the years to come, almost like Neil's voice calling for help and sanctuary for the birds he cared about so much.

It has continued to ring since then and has rung throughout the records kept by Peggy at the hospital. As Bell is her surname perhaps it has given her a sense of kinship! Here are some of her memories of Neil's bell:

Spring brings constant work for the bell, as the nestlings start to arrive. Gull babies fall off roofs, owl babies fall from barn rafters, even from church towers; house martins' nests fall from the eaves and some babies just get lost, like small ducklings. But they all come, and a busy staff rush round feeding gaping mouths, looking under stones for insects and worms or gathering moss from the walls, or sticks for tiny claws to perch on.

In Answer to the Cry

The bell sees the arrival of some strange patients: three baby shrews; a hedgehog who fell in the oil sump at a garage and was rushed up by a mechanic in a break-down van to be de-oiled. He was later released.

The bell has seen the fox, the seal pups and grown seals who are brought up these steps to be cared for; stray dogs, cats, and even once a child, who was quickly claimed. The fox brought to us had broken his brush and half of his pride and joy had to be amputated. Weeks later, he was released on the cliffs with a quick pat on the rump and a word of advice, 'Off you go and don't get into trouble; the hunt will never know you now.'

The bell did not ring that awful day when the *Torrey Canyon* sank. Birds were brought in in thousands, but there were no hands with time enough to ring bells. I am sure the bell rang silently though; maybe the hand of St Francis rested on it, as he suffered to see the death and destruction caused by man.

The bell saw at that time the postman staggering up the steps with bags of mail, as letters and donations poured in to the hospital from all over the world. Slowly the oil was fought, but it was never quite conquered. It rises up in a small way as ships are careless, or the sea still spews up a slick from the *Torrey Canyon* wreck. Even now, at the time of writing there is a Hull trawler aground on the rocks a few hundred yards from the hospital whose fate is still in doubt and which may have to be abandoned. Although her cargo was fish, not oil as with the *Torrey Canyon*, diesel oil and crude oil from the engines will probably seep into the sea, meaning that the bell will ring for yet more oiled birds. Now at the beginning of the year, the birds are coming into their territories around the coast preparatory to breeding. Many will never do so. This is just one wreck; there are countless others. So capricious are the currents, and our rocky coastline, that few ships that are wrecked on our shores ever sail away.

The bell hangs there and waits. It is not always shiny for there is not much time to polish bells. Cages have to be cleaned, birds

The Bell Still Rings

cared for, fed and comforted; but there is always a pair of hands to accept a newcomer.

Neil's bell has a rival; it sits on the office table and its shrill summons calls staff from runs and cages to speak to people who need problems solved. Advice is given, arrangements made, treatments discussed. Telephone calls come from places as far apart as the Isle of Man and the Isles of Scilly. It rings to say that birds are being sent by train, bus, or helicopter. One oiled gannet was picked up in the sea and arrived on the decks of a Scottish fishing trawler. A puffin rescued from the Seven Stones out at sea was brought to us having been saved by a fishing boat. A gull arrived by train from Wales, none the worse for his long journey. He was fed and joined other gulls in the run. Police stations ring to ask if we have a lost bird, or can we care for a lost budgie or parrot that has been found. Policemen often bring birds that they find on their travels, perhaps a northern diver or a gull.

The bell rings: a box is delivered at the hospital from a shop in St Ives. A man had come into the shop, put a box on the counter, and walked out, with no explanation. Inside the box was a heap of stinking feathers and twisted limbs. A pitiful sight, and we felt that there was little hope for this poor crow. Obviously the bird had been reared by someone who had kept it in a very confined space and fed it on the wrong food, so that its legs were weak and twisted and the feathers malformed. One beady little eye looked at us and deliberately winked, a beak gently tapped the hand holding him. Stinker, as he was christened, had won his first victory.

He who had never had a bath before was bathed and dried, fed and put in a warm place, given vitamins and his legs massaged. As the days went by he repaid us with his entertaining ways. He was re-named Tinker. His greatest delight was his big, airy house. Any attempt to remove him from it resulted in a raucous display of fury, a bristling of all his feathers and sharp pecks. He was given shiny tins to amuse him and little bits of cheese and biscuit were accepted and tucked away in corners of his 'home'.

In Answer to the Cry

He would never be able to be released as he had no flight feathers, but he was always such a happy little bird. All day long he surveyed new arrivals from his open door, and 'sweet-talked' the staff, while sharing their lunch. One visitor to Mousehole lost his heart to Tinker and came up almost daily just to have a word with him.

He would move around his house with a funny little hop, skip and jump, but we knew that his legs could never be straight. Summer came and he moulted. He looked awful, but gradually fluff started to grow and then feathers, preened carefully every day by Tinker and encouraged by remarks like, 'You are *beautiful*', from the staff.

The feathers were still badly formed but were shiny, and after all beauty is in the eye of the beholder. For two years we were greeted each morning by a cheerful 'squawk', and a sleepy 'good-night' every evening as a bright beady eye slowly closed in a head tucked under a half-wing.

A morning came when there was no greeting. He was greatly missed, but we had given him two happy years and he had repaid us with his mischievous antics and his cheerfulness had been a lesson to us all. In his condition there was nothing, one would have thought, to give him happiness of any kind. But misshapen though he was, and so badly cared for in the past, he still got so much from *living* and gave his affection freely; and he will always remain alive in our memories.

The bell pealed once for a sparrow hawk, brought to us from a field in Gulval just inland from Penzance. She had a pulled, strained wing, and we were able to assure her rescuers that she would be fit to return to freedom in about four weeks. The wing responded well, but the bird was nervous and distressed, spending long hours looking out at the world beyond the wire of her house. But the day came when we were sure the wing had recovered with all the strength needed by a bird of prey. She was put into a basket and taken to Gulval village, where her rescuers waited to point out

'If you can awaken a child's awareness of suffering it will last all through life and develop into an awareness of *all* suffering. Isn't that the only hope for the world?'

Immature gannet, came oiled, now ready for release.

Swan recovering.

Olga awaiting permission from a gannet.

'I'll soon get better' – Pam holding a barn owl with broken wing.

Gannet before cleansing.

Two gannets ready for freedom after cleansing from oil.

Gannets released to freedom again.

the field where she had been found, and to share with us the pleasure in her release.

The basket was opened and she was placed carefully on the ground beside it. She fluffed her feathers and looked around but stayed perfectly still. Suddenly she rose up and soared over the field in a wide circle; and as she did so another sparrow hawk swooped over the hedge and joined her as she completed the circle. They flew off together into a grove of trees. The other hawk must have been her mate who had waited all these long weeks for her return.

These are some of the records of the ringing of the bell – not all of them, but enough to show how the warden and her staff carry on the traditions of the sanctuary since we handed over, in a selfless and dedicated way.

In 1959 when Neil Jager would have been twenty-one years old, his parents sent a gift in loving remembrance of the child who by now would have grown to manhood.

This gift was spent on a very badly needed shallow bath in the grass run, for ducklings and wading birds. A tablet was put up with these words on it:

'Bird bath given May 29th 1959
when Neil Jager would have been 21.'

So once again he lives in all our thoughts and is still helping the birds.

Two of our old inhabitants, one an oyster catcher, the other a whimbrel, who had been rescued from death several years before, were the first to enjoy this bathing pool. Pog and I moved them there from the run they had shared with Dolly the Duck, when they first came, and where they had been supremely content under her influence. We called her our 'psychiatric matron' as she really had the gift of calming down nervous birds who were put with her on their arrival. But at her death they missed her, and we thought the lovely new bath and grass run would prove a consolation. This was so, and they soon settled happily in their new quarters.

Dolly's story is told in my first book. She had been brought all the way from Slough by a most caring couple who had rescued her after one of her wings had been hopelessly smashed by a stone thrown by some boys. They made a pond in their garden and kept her for two years, loving her dearly. But finally they decided she needed a companion so brought her all the way here to us.

She at once formed a great attachment to Pog and lived in Pog's hut with a good run, in which she made a special bath for her. There was a very real friendship between them and Dolly would follow Pog about everywhere.

The sad day eventually came when Dolly began to fail and show her age. Her feathers got thin and her zest for life waned. We took her down to Green Hedges and made a warm quiet corner for her in our bird room there. She was content, seemed to know that life held no more for her, and quietly slept most of the time, till one morning she wakened no more.

We missed her greatly.

May Neil's bell long continue to ring as evidence of the compassion in the hearts of those who ring it.

XII

From Far and Near

The majority of our patients are local to Cornwall, but we have always received quite a number of birds from much further afield. However the local birds have many differing problems, some of which can be quite out of the ordinary as the girls have found:

Whilst an oil pollution disaster can bring to the hospital in one week hundreds of members of the auk family, mainly guillemots and razorbills, it is the gulls who are regularly one of the most prolific in number amongst our patients. They range from the formidable greater black back down to the dove-sized little gull. In between come the lesser black back, herring, common and black headed gulls and the pretty kittiwake.

Gulls are victims of all sorts of misadventures. We have had them brought with broken legs and wings, tangled in fishing hooks or lines, shot, knocked down by cars, hit by a train, oiled, and battered by gales. In fact we thought we had encountered every hazard known to the species until one September some visitors found an adult herring gull staggering along a Penzance street.

'We know it sounds incredible,' they told us, 'but we think it's *drunk!*'

The bleary-eyed gull was set down on the office floor and promptly tottered forwards on to its beak. It was put back on its feet and in doing so we noticed its breath did indeed reek of spirits.

In Answer to the Cry

There was no doubt about it, the gull was one over the eight. All we could do was put it in a quiet cage to sleep off its excesses.

One inebriated gull was hard enough to believe but when *three more* were brought to us in the next couple of days, it began to look as though we were coping with a problem of bacchanalian proportions. To add to the drama, one of these gulls was actually 'arrested' by Penzance police for being drunk and disorderly. This poor bird was to give us the clue to the source of the intoxication. It was in a very bad way, reeling and rolling about in great distress. At last it vomited a mess of currants and other waste which emitted the unmistakable odour of strong alcohol. We guessed this gull (and probably the others) had come across the thrown out, fermented remains of home wine-making and gorged itself into a stupor.

True to the tradition of the morning-after-the-night-before, the hung-over gulls winced at every noise but, fortunately, they suffered no permanent harm and were soon released as once more sober and upright members of the bird community.

More worrying, over the last two years, has been the admittance of herring, black headed and greater black back gulls, afflicted by what are believed to be the poisonous effects of pollution. They are brought to us chiefly in the hot summer months and have come to be called the 'Lurgy Gulls'. To a lesser or greater degree, they all display similar symptoms; paralysis of the legs and wings, breathing difficulties and enteritis. Some are so ill we have almost given them up for dead but the recovery rate is high even amongst the sickest birds.

For the first twenty-four hours the gull is semi-conscious. It wants no food but will drink a little water into which a small dose of Aureomycin has been put. The next day it may begin to show signs of returning to normality by eating little pieces of fish and also may try to stand but completely lacks muscle co-ordination. In another two days it will have found its unsteady feet and from that point on its recovery is assured. It takes about ten days for a

From Far and Near

Lurgy Gull to recover and by this time it will be flying round the run or even 'battering' to go. The only clue we have to the source of pollution is that the majority of these birds have come from the St Ives and Hayle estuaries.

An exclusively herring gull problem, which the hospital has to face each year, is the constant stream of youngsters admitted that have fallen from roof-top nests. They are brought between June and August and range in age from fluffy speckled chick straight out of the egg, to gangling 'teenager' or the nearly fully fledged 'apprentice flier'.

For many years we had several pairs of permanently injured gulls who each year built nests, mated and laid their eggs. All but one of these eggs were pricked and when this fertile egg was hatched it was possible to foster several orphaned babies with each pair, so long as they were approximately the same size as 'junior'. We regret the passing of our 'working patients', who have now all died of old age.

The number of herring gulls that have chosen to build their nests in coastal towns and villages has increased alarmingly over recent years. Unfortunately, the noise and mess they create has brought them into conflict with the human residents and summer visitors. Yet the gulls perform a valuable service in scavenging the beaches and harbours. And, is it their fault if they are encouraged to stay by those who use them as convenient 'dustbins' to dispose of unwanted food scraps? The hospital may come under criticism for helping to rear so many orphaned youngsters but they are brought here both in need of help and out of the compassion of their rescuers. Are we to discriminate between the species of birds that come into our care?

Last year some 150 young gulls were reared to releasable state and the question of where to let them go became of paramount importance. After a great deal of thought, we decided to release them straight into their natural environment on the cliffs far away from habitation. This has proved so successful it has now become hospital policy and has provided new experiences in the returning of captivity-reared birds back into the wild.

The Atlantic coast between Land's End and Gurnard's Head must be one of the wildest parts of a land steeped in legend and history, where the very beginning of time has left its mark as the earth cooled and precious metals were formed. Man was to risk his life to wrest these treasures from the earth and, in doing so, altered the very shape of parts of this coast. He left behind deep fissures and 'zowns' in the cliff as he relentlessly followed the rich veins of copper and tin.

Nature has covered much of these marks of man. Gorse, heather and brambles grow in abundance and spring brings carpets of wild scilla, primroses and violets on and around the ruins of the old mine workings, while sea pinks and ferms provide ledges on which the coastal birds build their nests. Bird-life abounds here. Shags and cormorants preen on the flat rocks at the foot of the cliffs, gulls fish for their food, whilst near the ruins of mine chimneys, rooks, crows and jackdaws chatter and swoop around their nests.

This then was the part of the Cornish coast that came to mind when the serious business was up for discussion on the release of our immature gulls, because we felt it was essential that they did not become 'roof-top gulls' like their parents.

Each day a dozen youngsters were separated from their fellows before feeding time. The reason for this was that if they ate a full feed they would be over-loaded to take off on their first major flight. This problem does not occur in the wild as the birds' diet is adjusted by the amount of food available and their parents' good sense. In the afternoon they were placed in the van and driven to where rough tracks lead across the wild land to the cliff tops. The doors were opened and the young gulls were allowed to make their own way out whilst their human attendant settled in a sheltered spot, for the long wait that was to follow.

At first the gulls wandered around pulling at bits of heather and surveying their new world of sea and cliffs. Then little runs were taken and wings stretched. Soon one youngster actually left the ground, rather wobbly and forgetting to tuck his legs up. In no time at all the excitement spread and they were all airborne, coping with uplift and air pockets on wings they had only used before in restricted flight. They glided, banked and whirled taking short trips over the sea, coming back each time to land with more confidence.

Great apprehension was felt by their 'nursemaids' as, an hour later, a flock of local gulls arose screaming from their cliff ledges and circled the air above the 'babies'. But the 'locals' merely settled on nearby rocks to watch the flying lessons with bright critical eyes. Soon we were amazed to see them joining in the trial flights. They even chased away a noisy crowd of crows and jackdaws that came to investigate what all the activity was about. After an hour or so our youngsters were escorted to the cliff ledges and it was a relief to know their new friends had almost literally taken them under their wings. Darkness was nearly complete by this time and suddenly the heather was lit by dozens of small lights. The glow-worms had 'switched on'. This wonderful sight does not happen every year but, once seen, is never forgotten. Each afternoon more young gulls were released in the same way, and we lingered on to see the glow-worms until one night there was nothing. We waited until the moon rose and turned the sea to silver but the glow-worms' courtship was over.

Early each morning we came back to the cliff top with a bowl of mackerel in case our birds needed help with their breakfast and to make sure that all was well. But the offer of fish was ignored and not one of our babies could be seen on the cliff where they had taken their first flight into the outside world.

There is a special gull character at the hospital whom we would love to see take to the wing one day. He is a greater black back, now in his third year with us, and his name is Albert Ross. He was 'christened' quite unconsciously by a small boy who spent all one morning diligently observing the birds in our care. At last he plucked up courage to talk to us and asked, 'Where did you get your albatross from?'

This was intriguing news to us. 'We haven't got an albatross,' we told him.

'Oh yes you have! He's there in the run.' He pointed to the greater black back, who up to that time had been known as the Featherless Wonder.

That description is rather unkindly inaccurate because the bird has perfect plumage on his head, neck and front. But his wings and rear view are a total disaster. The long flight feathers refuse to grow and his tail end has a decidedly 'blasted' appearance.

We were so amused by the Featherless Wonder's promotion to 'albatross' that the name stuck and eventually evolved into the Albert Ross of today. Each morning we look at him hopefully for signs of a full set of feathers beginning to sprout but so far Albert has failed to produce more than an embarrassment-saving fluff.

As is to be expected, the majority of our birds come from this county. However, we often receive reassurances that word of the hospital and its work has spread much further afield.

There is a lady in Wales who has quite regularly sent us injured birds to convalesce. They arrive in carefully prepared travelling boxes, always with an envelope taped to the inside containing a pound note to help towards the bird's keep. One Welsh patient was Gloria the gannet. She had been heavily oiled and when she arrived her plumage was still badly stained. But she had stood the journey well and with a few days' rest was strong enough to face a second wash. We had the great satisfaction of releasing her with four Cornish gannets a month or so later and they all went off together beautifully.

In fact oiled birds seem to rather predominate the patients sent from afar. Perhaps because their re-habilitation requires special facilities and sometimes weeks of patient care, which we are able to give. There is no short cut to complete recovery although much has been learnt about cleaning them. Moreover, we have strong reason to believe that the very trauma of being taken out of their natural environment and subjected to so much initial, though unavoidable, handling are additional reasons for the delay in their becoming waterproof. Proof of this lies in the fact that we care for many sea birds that have not been oiled, and therefore are not washed. Yet they too can lose their waterproofing when first admitted to the hospital and only regain it when they are settled, and on the road to recovery. So the oiled bird has a double battle to fight.

During the pollution off the coast of Scotland last year, we came into regular correspondence with a lady, living in the county of Sutherland, who needed advice about the oiled birds she had rescued. She decided she had not sufficient facilities to cope with their after-care and asked if we would accept her surviving birds. The two guillemots and one razorbill travelled to Penzance on the overnight train and settled in with our own small colony of convalescing birds.

Two more Scottish patients, fulmars, arrived from Inverness last autumn, brought by the kind people who had looked after them. These large-eyed, grey and white birds are sometimes mistaken for gulls but they have the raised, tubular nostrils characteristic of the petrel family to which they belong. They also have the rather unpleasant habit of spitting a foul-smelling orange liquid as a defensive measure. Our fulmars were contrasting characters. One seemed somewhat frail and elderly but the other one was a bustling, robust fellow. The 'old gentleman' died peacefully in his sleep a week after his admittance. However, a fortnight later, his companion was taken to the cliff tops for release. In the same way as gannets, the fulmar has to be launched from a height to catch the uplift of air and this one glided off happily on straight wings to join a 'sassenach' fulmar colony near-by.

In Answer to the Cry

Perhaps the most illustrious patient of recent times who came from afar was a young cormorant from Bournemouth. To save him the tedium of the long road journey, this well-heeled character was flown in a private plane, generously laid on by his rescuers, to tiny St Just airport, about nine miles away. From there the two gentlemen who had looked after him so splendidly chauffeured him to Mousehole. 'His Lordship' arrived complete with a small supply of sprats and we were told he would eat nothing else. Such luxuries are hard to come by here, but fortunately the cormorant deigned to agree that whole Cornish mackerel were quite acceptable and had the added bonus that they filled him much more rapidly than sprats.

Cormorants, like their smaller relative the shag, are one of the few diving birds whose plumage gets wet after long spells in water. Hence they can often be seen standing on rocks by the shore, with their wings 'hung out to dry'. This characteristic pose has been captured to perfection in the beautiful wooden carving of a shag which adorns one of the collecting boxes at the hospital. His Lordship's problem was that his feathers soaked up water like a sponge the instant he entered the pond and he had to come out to dry within a couple of minutes. However his water-resistance improved daily and he took great delight in diving to the bottom of the deep pond for the fish we threw to him.

At last we decided he was fit for release and Peggy took him down to the beach below the hospital. He thought a stroll over the rocks was a rather jolly idea and tagged behind Peggy who had to show him the way to the sea. She was so concentrating on the bird flip-flopping behind her she did not realise the sea had become rather close, took another step forward and found the rocks had ended and the waves had begun. From this, albeit unintentional, practical demonstration His Lordship got the message and dived off into the water.

A week later he was back with us, having attached himself to some local children playing near the harbour. Thinking the

From Far and Near

cormorant was in need of help, they picked him up and proudly presented him at the office door. He seemed very hungry but none the worse for his first sojourn in the wild.

Soon he was fit again and this time it was decided to take him to Newlyn harbour, where it was hoped he would join the resident shags. We had a word with our good friends at the fish suppliers there and they promised to keep an eye on the bird. Two days later Peggy went back to check on his progress and was told that the cormorant had indeed joined the shags, but only for a day; the following morning he had been seen flying strongly around the harbour. In the afternoon he had vanished, apparently deciding to seek pastures new.

In contrast to the stories of the birds who have come from afar is that of a magpie. She became one of the very few patients that we have entrusted to a private home. And now, she lives far from the ring of Neil's bell and her old friends at the hospital.

Maggie was brought in some four years ago, a young hand-reared bird and much too tame to release. We hoped in time that she would become wild but she in fact got tamer as the years went by. Little Maggie was thoroughly domesticated and could never adjust to the wild.

The staff were greeted every day with chirps of welcome when they went into the run to clean it, and Maggie would sit on a shoulder to gently tweak an ear or pull a lock of hair, while she waited for the fresh water to run into the pond for her bath. She was quite happy with the pigeons and collared doves who shared the aviary with her. We soon noticed she loved children and she could be heard laughing and talking to the young visitors who came to see us.

This affection became even more evident on one occasion when she accidentally got out of her aviary. She flew down to the village and spent the day on the harbour with the children. To get her back they had only to walk up the hill and Maggie followed. They came up to the hospital steps and we were able to take her in, very

In Answer to the Cry

hungry but very happy. This episode told us that Maggie really needed the company of children and would be perhaps more happy in a private home with a family who could give her all their attention and love. And so it was decided that if ever we could find such a family we would let her go to them. We had many offers but none ever came to anything; either we were not satisfied that the people were sincere enough or the accommodation was not right. So, we were quite happy to keep Maggie indefinitely, that is until the summer of this year.

One morning a husband and wife with their two children came to visit the hospital. They spent a long while looking around and chatting to the staff and even longer chatting to Maggie. After a while the husband came to the office to ask about her and was told her story and how we hoped one day to find a home for her. He listened and then said, 'Would you let us give Maggie a home? We have all fallen for her and have a house and aviary nearly as big as the one she is in now. To ease your mind I will send you a photo of the aviary when I get back.'

We immediately recognised the sincerity of his offer, but because of the distance between his home and the hospital, we hesitated to give him a final answer until we had seen the photographs.

The family returned to Gravesend. A week passed and the photograph arrived with a letter offering to meet the train in London, if Maggie was dispatched from Penzance. We all agreed it was a wonderful chance for the bird, but were worried about her travelling the long distance in the hot weather. We phoned to explain all this and the result was that her departure was postponed.

Autumn came and the weather at last cooled. One weekend she was placed in a specially prepared travelling box. It had a firm perch, a night-blind and on the top was written the message 'Bon Voyage Maggie'. At ten o'clock in the evening, she started her long journey in the hospital van with the member of staff who was driving through the night to meet Maggie's new family. They had arranged to drive part of the way through Surrey to make a rendezvous early the next morning.

Maggie slept for most of the journey and ate an early breakfast of cheese and half a sausage roll that had been given her as a parting present. Her new family as arranged arrived to meet her and she greeted the children with chirps of joy. The last that was seen of her was a flash of beautiful plumage as she settled happily into the family car. It would indeed be lonely without our little friend, we knew we would all miss her but there would always be other birds to care for. Before the hospital van had returned to Mousehole, a reassuring phone call had been received to say that Maggie was settled and happy in her new home.

Later, we received fuller details of her journey. After she had been put in the car, to begin with all was quiet within the travelling box. Then suddenly, from inside, a little voice piped up with a hesitant 'Hello'. The children instantly responded and 'Helloes' passed back and forth until Maggie burst into her infectious giggle. The rest of the trip home was completed to the accompaniment of peels of laughter from bird and humans alike.

We heard too that Maggie approved of her new quarters, a spacious aviary and indoor house. Soon she had sorted out favourite hiding places for her food stores and intrigued the family with her habit of washing her food before eating it. She adored the children and they spent a lot of time in the aviary with her so that she could perch on their arms and chatter away to her heart's content. All this news reinforced our belief that the decision to say farewell to our friend had been justified and we now look forward to receiving the promised photos of her in her new life at Gravesend.

It warmed our hearts that yet again we had come across such caring people who were willing and happy to go to so much trouble for the sake of a bird in need. There are, we know, important reasons for the work we do but it is often the small and touching things that bring home to us how worthwhile it all is.

XIII
Our Crisis Year

In the January of 1975 we tried to remind ourselves of what an old friend had once said to us, 'If you want to go on, you must go slow.' The years were catching up on us; Pog was eighty-three and I was eighty-five. We did try and cut down a bit physically, but mentally we could not surrender to old age. There was still so much to be done.

Then, in the first week of that New Year, the bombshell fell.

One morning a letter came giving us the unbelievable news that the RSPCA, for financial reasons, were going to close the Birds' Hospital the very next month, on 28th February, and were sending officials down to instruct the staff as to the destruction of the birds, except for any we personally might wish to keep.

'Closed!' Pog and I were stunned. For forty-seven years the door of the sanctuary had always been open; and now? *No*, it could not be. 'Better to fail at the impossible than to succeed at the obvious.' These words came to my mind, something I had read long ago and never forgotten.

But *how* was it to be done? We had very little money. We were too old to work any more. Then, in a flash, I suddenly thought of the £500 we had set aside in the bank for a rainy day. This was indeed the rainy day, and it could tide us over. This was a miracle. We knew how to answer that fatal letter.

First I went up to the hospital to tell the staff of our plan. They too had received this shattering letter and were horrified. I asked

Our Crisis Year

them if they would support Pog and me if we undertook to maintain the hospital from 28th February, paying all expenses from week to week, until we could see some hope for the future? Their faces lightened, and with one voice they agreed to stand by us and the birds whatever happened.

Going back to the quiet of the studio, Pog and I had a final talk as to the task ahead. It ended with Pog saying in her direct way, 'Well, if we *have* to climb the Himalayas, then we *must* climb the Himalayas.' The decision had been made. Our letter was sent by return of post to the RSPCA stating that we accepted the financial reasons they gave for ceasing to run the hospital, but would they please *not* close down on 28th February, but leave everything exactly as it was, and we would undertake all responsibility from that day. If we failed in the end it would be no worse than their failure on 28th February.

What next? Directly the Society made a public announcement on the radio the news spread like wildfire. The girls were constantly called to the telephone, answering questions, 'What has happened?' 'Where do we take the birds now?', all expressing anxiety.

Then, within a few days, we had a visit from a local Justice of the Peace who lived in Mousehole. His wife's grandparents had been amongst our earliest friends in the village; the links were holding. Almost his first words were, 'This must not happen', and later 'We must call a public meeting'. Our breath was taken away; help had started to come; the miracle was beginning to work. Owing to his untiring efforts we had a 'full house' at the meeting in the village, which resulted in a committee being formed with our kind friend as the Chairman; an Hon Secretary and Hon Treasurer offered their services and were appointed. A Penzance solicitor volunteered to be our Hon Legal Adviser, and they were kind enough to ask me to be the President. A real beginning had been made.

Within two days of the news of the proposed closure of the sanctuary, the press also came to our aid. The local newspaper *The*

In Answer to the Cry

Cornishman wrote a helpful appeal. Michael Moynihan of the *Sunday Times* rang me up from London to say he was coming down the next day, being concerned as to the future of the Birds' Hospital about which he had written a few years earlier. He actually stayed on, and came to that first committee meeting and gave a wonderful report of all that had happened in the next week's *Sunday Times*.

Donald Zec of the *Daily Mirror* also came down, talked to us for a very long time, and in a few days his full account of what was happening appeared in his paper and brought us instant and generous response.

The *Sunday Times* article reached Switzerland, where it was read by HRH the Aga Khan who wrote a personal letter to us saying he and his wife took pleasure in enclosing a cheque for £1,000 to help our struggle to save the Birds' Hospital and Sanctuary, and that he was sending the article on to HRH Prince Bernhardt of the Netherlands. Soon we received £500 from him with all his good wishes. How grateful we were for these almost unbelievable contributions.

But to come nearer home. The children of Mousehole were amongst the first to come to the rescue of 'their' hospital.

One day we heard a knock on the door of our cottage and there were four children, one small girl and three boys, aged between seven and nine I should think. They came in, lined up, and then one boy, the obvious leader said, 'We want you to come and draw the raffle tickets on Saturday when we are holding an exhibition of our drawings and selling things for the Birds' Hospital.' I thanked them, and asked their names. The leader said, 'Which do you want, our bird names or our real names?' 'Oh, both please,' said I.

Then the leader spoke:

'I am Matthew Halkes; my bird name is *Hawk*.
'My sister Becky's bird name is *Sparrow-Hawk*.
'Brian Ellis' bird name is *Eagle*.
'Michael Blewitt's bird name is *Blue-Tit*.'

Our Crisis Year

I went on the Saturday, Matthew received me at the entrance to the hall, and when I offered my five pence admission money he very courteously swept my hand aside and said, '*You* pay nothing'. They made over £60 that afternoon and later with sponsored walks round the school playground raised £200 that year.

Other schools from near and far followed with contributions, all raised by their own efforts. Football clubs, Guides, Brownies and Scouts all helped. The children were with us and would fight to the end to save the sanctuary. The local Salvation Army, Women's Institutes and many other public bodies held coffee mornings and gatherings of different sorts, in our aid.

From these sources we gained at least another £1,000 and further donations came from all over the country. The tide seemed to be turning indeed.

Many individual members of the RSPCA wrote expressing much regret at the society's having to withdraw its support, and they sent personal gifts.

Then, to start us off in 1976 came another marvellous £1,000, this time from the Staffordshire branch of the RSPCA whose Hon Secretary wrote that 'this money comes with the consent of the Council of the RSPCA hoping it is realised that the society still feels warmly towards your work'. This started a friendship with the secretary and her husband who later made a special visit to the sanctuary and came to one of our committee meetings, expressing real interest in everything.

The committee in the meantime were being very active in arranging flag days, collecting boxes, raffles, jumble sales and bringing out forms for all those who wished to contribute regularly as Friends of the Birds' Hospital.* A dress show was generously given by a Penzance Fashion House to help our funds. The Minack

---

*Publisher's Note. Any reader who might wish to support the hospital by enrolling as a Friend can obtain particulars from The Hon Secretary, Mousehole Wild Bird Hospital and Sanctuary, Mousehole, Penzance, Cornwall.

In Answer to the Cry

Theatre at nearby Porthcurno most kindly let us share in their Sunday collections for Charities.

All these efforts made on our behalf this first year of our 'independence', this 'new beginning', ended in triumph in our having paid our way, with enough in hand to go well on into our second year.

One of our 'miracles' at this time was the coming of the Free Fish era. A local fisherman brought a puffin he had rescued from an oil slick while at sea. He had put the poor mite into his warm woollen cap and brought it to the sanctuary. He was concerned to hear we had to pay for all the fish used and said he would talk to the other trawlermen and get them all to help with free fish when their catch allowed it, if it could be collected from the Newlyn Fish Market. So one of the staff went daily in the little hospital van to get this marvellous windfall.

One day *no* boats had been to sea. Peggy Bell, who had gone that morning, wandered disconsolately round the market, when a man came up and asked if she wanted anything. She explained. He was very sympathetic, and said he would arrange for his firm, Suttons Fish Wholesalers of Newlyn, to supply the sanctuary with free fish whenever needed. As it was a daily need for most of the year, this, in addition to the fishermen's generous help, was indeed a wonderful offer. How grateful the staff were for such an undreamt of solution to the ever-increasing problem caused by the rising price of fish.

Our second year began, as the year before, with encouraging help from the press. We had many letters and gifts as the result of an article in a newspaper for the elderly called *Yours*, which told of the struggle we were having to survive. They were touching letters, many just signed 'from an Old Age pensioner'. But in two months they had given our birds £200, in small amounts chiefly, which made them all the more valuable to us. We recognised the sacrifice they must have entailed.

I should like to share with you who are reading these pages

Our Crisis Year

something written in a letter we had about this time. It came from Hampshire with a generous donation for our funds for which we were very grateful. But what we shall always remember is the final part of this letter. Here it is:

> Perhaps you would like to hear this little story that is quite true because I was there. A thrush died, and was duly buried with much pomp by my three children, aged three, five and seven. The next day I watched from my window as they dug up the bird to see whether it had 'ascended into Heaven'. Great disappointment appeared to be expressed when the occupant was found still in the ceremonial cardboard burial box.
>
> There was a pause, and then a voice from the five-year-old, 'We *are* silly; it's only the *singing* part that goes to heaven.'

The child had spoken and we felt an echo of the thrush's song in our hearts as we thought of all those birds we had loved and who were with us no more.

XIV
The Lights Go On

The great event of this year of 1976 was when a member of our committee gave us an introduction to Sandra Wainwright of the BBC, who is the director of the television programme *Look Stranger*. She came down for a week in May with the well-known author and broadcaster, Rene Cutforth, and her team of camera men, sound recorders and assistants.

Pog and I were overwhelmed at the prospect and so were the girls, but we pulled ourselves together and thought — well, we can only do our best and hope it will not be too awful. But when one is faced with an ordeal of this kind some little incident often occurs which transforms the situation. In our case it was a robin.

The girls were getting all in order at the hospital, and Pog was making her studio slightly fit for the intruders (though she never cared much what people thought), clearing up the fireplace, making her bed, and putting one of the inscrutable eastern looking masks she had modelled, on to the pillow, with a sheet pulled up to his chin and a long cigarette holder with a fag in it, in his mouth. I was in the cottage desperately 'tidying up', and feeding the wild birds on the balcony and cleaning Peardrop's house etcetera.

Soon I heard voices, noisy sounds of a car being unloaded, and then footsteps. The minute had come. I went to receive the BBC but no! When I opened the door it was Bobbin the robin who was on the doorstep. He used our house as his own. He had forestalled

The Lights Go On

the officials, who had stopped dead when they saw him. I quickly leant down and presented him with his usual bit of cheese on the tip of my finger. He took his time and then flew off. Our visitors took not the slightest notice of me nor I of them. The ice was broken.

All the men had wanted was to set up the cameras inside the room, but now they asked me to stand in the doorway and call back Bobbin. This I did and he obliged; and they took a shot of us both.

The morning was spent with Sandra Wainwright rehearsing us all, in preparation for the arrival of Rene Cutforth. She was wonderful, giving us an idea of the questions we must be ready to answer, and the men were busy finding the right places for their cameras and lights and other equipment. We then went up to the studio and reached it as Pog opened the door. The first thing they saw was the mask tucked up to the chin in her bed. They told us afterwards they had been quite taken in and for a second felt really embarrassed! Once more the ice was broken; everyone laughed and enjoyed the joke.

They much admired her carvings and took several pictures, including one of her at the window feeding Tapper the rook, who had been reared at the hospital a few years before. Though now completely adapted to wild life he never forgot Pog but came daily to the studio, knocking on her window at dawn.

With Rene Cutforth there was never any ice to break. He was so kind and courteous, putting us at our ease at once, and our interviews flowed along as if we were talking to an old friend.

The cameras and flashing lights were forgotten. One lovely thing happened which I hardly noticed at the time. Our little Peardrop, who was still with us then, was determined not to be outdone by the BBC and from his own 'house' by my bed continued his full May song at intervals as usual. When September came and the film was shown on television Pog and I were rather nervously looking at the programme when we suddenly heard this beautiful little voice letting the whole nation know how content he

In Answer to the Cry

was in his sanctuary. Many friends wrote saying, 'Was that Peardrop we heard?' They could hardly believe it.

The warden and staff at the hospital co-operated with enthusiasm. A very long time was spent up there and pictures taken showing every aspect of their work. This included the cleaning of an oiled bird, treatment being given to a casualty on arrival, and the various species in residence, including Jimmy, our oldest bird.

Wonderful coverage was given in this film. The cameras were taken to the Mousehole School where the children and I had a talk together about the birds they had brought to the hospital.

Having left the school the team visited our Mousehole Ship Inn where the chairman and members of our committee told of the value the sanctuary was to the village, and local fishermen spoke of their support of it over many years. They spoke too of the help the gulls bring to them in showing where the shoals of fish are, and how when there is a thick fog they listen for the birds' cries which warn them rocks are near.

There were beautiful scenes taken of Mousehole with its lovely background of hills, and finally one down on the rocks, showing the happy release of several guillemots, previously oiled, but now fit and well, completely ready for freedom.

We can never thank Sandra Wainwright and Rene Cutforth enough for making this *Look Stranger* programme in such a perfect way.

September came. The film was shown; and the day after the letters started pouring in. Twenty a day sometimes; many writers in such a hurry to tell us how they had enjoyed it that they recklessly sent by first class post! That really pleased us. The generous gifts that came with them to help the survival of our sanctuary amazed us.

One arrived that first week anonymously, with only the postmark, *Luton*, giving a clue as to the sender. Inside was a small bit of paper enclosing a £1 note with the words 'Good Luck!!!'.

The Lights Go On

This has come *every week* since that 14th September until this very day – over a year and no sign of it stopping. So if that is worked out it can be seen what a generous and faithful friend the birds have in Luton. How I hope he or she may by chance see this page and know what this kind thought has meant to us.

Still the letters reached us and by the end of the sixth week we had received £1,000! And perhaps, best of all, everyone wanted our sanctuary to carry on; it was so badly needed on our long Cornish coast.

The next big event was when our committee decided to hold a Christmas Bazaar in Penzance for the Birds' Hospital. How the staff worked for it! Olga, Peggy and Pam never ceased making articles to sell and kept collecting gifts offered by local shops who all gave most generously. A splendid effort, all done after hours, when their work with the birds was finished for the day.

Many 'Friends of the Hospital' from all over the country also sent woollen hand-knitted garments, toys, sweets and other things to sell. The reward was great, because, in spite of rather bad weather, the attendance on the day was wonderful and £500 was raised.

Through the year many kind people who love birds and are happy about the work being done here, helped in their various ways, sending for instance a piece of jewellery, an old gold watch, a brooch, a silk oriental wall-covering, and one anonymous donor gave a beautiful old necklace, all of which must have meant a lot to them.

Another special day came in October, when, thanks to the great efforts made by our Hon Legal Adviser, the Birds' Hospital became a registered charity. He had told us in the beginning that this would be necessary before we could consider the possibility of trying to find sponsorship from one of the big oil companies or other public firms. If *only* we could get a good response of this kind that would bring enough capital to ensure the permanent life of our sanctuary, how thankful we should all be.

In Answer to the Cry

I am sure, when faced with the horror of pollution, the public conscience is moved by the thought that we are all involved in the use of oil in our daily needs and therefore we *must* find a way of atoning, in however slight a degree, for the suffering of the completely innocent victims, the birds of the sea.

XV
Wise Old Owls and Strong-minded Gannets

When the hectic days of the broadcasting and money-raising schemes were over, but of course only for the moment, our thoughts turned once more for refreshment to the birds, who take no thought for the morrow but wisely accept life as it comes, conserving their energies for the problems that may confront them. Our problems for the future were formidable but we had to carry on.

Two baby tawny owls had been found, when only one or two weeks old, on the Truro Golf Course by one of the members. He took them in to the stewardess of the clubhouse, Mrs Barber, who fell for them at once. They were weak and helpless, but in three days her intensive care was rewarded by the little ones taking on a new lease of life and beginning to pick up food for themselves.

All the club members had taken on enormous interest in the babies, and it was decided it would be best to send them over to Mousehole until they were ready for release. This was in May, the busiest month of the year at the hospital with its annual influx of baby birds. So as the staff were desperately occupied, Pog and I said we would look after them at home.

We prepared a big dove cage in the corner of our sitting-room where they settled in at once. We called them Bumble and Bee. Bumble was slightly larger than Bee. They were devoted to each other and accepted us as providers of food which they took readily from our fingers. This consisted of a mash of Sluice, finely chopped meat or rabbit, a little vitamin powder, and small feathers and rabbit fur to give them some roughage. The mixture seemed to suit, because three days later we found two pellets on the ground which showed us that their digestive systems were working properly.

They slept peacefully after their breakfast for most of the day. Then when evening came, we opened the door of their house and they at once perched on the bough at the entrance, side by side, slowly considering what to do next. At first it was a short flight to the back of a chair, and quick return to their 'cottage home', then in three weeks they were making short flights round the room, sitting on the mantelpiece and finally on to the couch which they loved with its soft landing of cushions. Here we fixed up a tray with pans of water in which they could have their daily bath. Bumble particularly enjoyed this.

When about six weeks old their feathers were growing beautifully, replacing the furry down of their babyhood, and their flight was very strong and swift; so we took them back to the hospital where they were put in a big loft to complete their 'growing up'.

In the meantime the member of the Golf Club who had rescued them, had been over and was delighted with their progress. He said he would prepare a shed on the links where they could be kept for a short time until they could be released near the place in which he had found them.

Two weeks later the great day came. We took them over by car, placed their house on the seat beside us, and when all the windows were shut, we opened their door where they sat like royalty at the entrance, never moving for the whole long journey to Truro except to turn their heads from side to side to observe the view.

When we arrived all the club members were assembled to receive them and escorted them to their new quarters. Inside was a table on which the house was stood, with bath and food pans all ready and beautiful boughs placed all over the shed. Their kind friend, Mrs Barber, was there to wait on them. Much to her joy they seemed to remember her and were completely 'at home' again. She rang us up a few weeks later to say Bumble and Bee were fully grown and perfectly fit, so they had once more been escorted by the members to the wooded part of the links near where they had been found and the door was opened. This time, no sitting on the doorstep but instant flight to the trees.

Every evening about 9 p.m. they returned to Mrs Barber's whistle and Bumble would sit on her arm, while Bee would perch on a bough near by. Gradually they came less and less often, and by the end of the summer had re-joined the wild life from which they came.

Every year the hospital gets many owls to care for. As Peggy tells:

The nestlings arrive from mid May onwards, little bundles of fluff, their big eyes gazing out on a bewildering world. They fall from church towers, or are stolen from nests. Hollow trees get felled and nests are found within. All the time the hazards are greater as parents are shot or poisoned through eating prey contaminated by insecticides. They are good friends of man, as they live on small creatures which ruin the farmer's crops, and the barn owls protect the farmer's stores from mice and other rodents.

The beautiful barn owl with its heart-shaped mask and fantastic range of colour-tones in his patterned feathers is a marvellous creature that no picture can do justice to. No wonder he gets associated with ghostly things as he flies on his silent wings in the near dark. There is no sound of his flight, for nature gave him powerful wings that grow in such a way that the feathers *lift* and air flows *through* them, unlike those of other birds, that are formed to *hold* them on the currents of air.

These birds grow quickly and soon learn to feed themselves from scraps of raw meat, fur and rabbit. We watch them carefully in the hospital, and there is a great sigh of relief when they make their first pellet. This means they are normal and healthy little birds. Their digestive system is such that small bones and hard objects are stored, and acid from the bird's body breaks them down and they are formed into a pellet which is regurgitated. Thus there is no damage to the bird's inner stomach.

We keep these young ones for a few weeks in the bird room next to the office where their mysterious personality causes both pleasure and wonder to our many visitors and school parties. When all their fluff has moulted out and they have a complete set of new feathers and they are old enough to 'pull' their own food, they are moved up into the loft where they learn to use their wings.

Once up there they revert to being completely wild, over-night. The rather dependent little creatures who can be handled with ease and who perch on tops of doors or even shoulders, now fly away from you and 'tick' angrily if approached too closely during our daily cleaning. A week or so more and they are taken for release to a kind friend of the hospital, who lives in a cottage half way down the beautiful wooded valley that leads to Lamorna Cove, a few miles away. She looks after the youngsters and feeds them for several days in a shed. Then one night she opens the door, still leaving food for them inside so that they can return until they adapt into the wild. She was delighted to find that there is now a small colony of these birds settled in the trees above the little stream that rushes down to the sea nearby. Nevertheless we have had some quite hectic experiences with owls.

We received a phone call one day from the vicarage at Newlyn asking if one of us could possibly come along and cope with an owl which had flown into the dining-room through the top of the tall windows. These faced onto the Coombe, where tall elm trees grow beside the river that runs down into the Newlyn Harbour. The housekeeper was an elderly lady and she was terrified of birds. Entering the dining-room she was startled when a bundle of feathers fluttered across the room, narrowly missing some porcelain displayed on the sideboard. The bird landed in a corner of the room where it sat, its large eyes gazing at its unfamiliar surroundings. The lady fled, leaving the owl in sole occupation, and this was the situation that confronted the Vicar on his return.

He rang us because, when he opened the door of the dining-room, he realised that the bird was distressed and would not fly away on its own accord, and he was concerned that it might come to harm if it was panicked.

When I arrived I was shut in the room with the tawny owl who was nowhere to be seen. I found it huddled in a corner, under the sideboard. A bundle of ruffled feathers 'ticking' and hissing with fright and rage as I tried to crawl into the narrow space between the sideboard and floor to reach him. The owl decided to come out as I was almost within reach, and so we confronted each other under the table. He stood there, his sharp claws digging into the carpet, every feather on end, big eyes glaring at me as he brought his wings up to meet behind his head in 'fanning' display.

Relying on what I hoped to be fact, that although tawny owls come out in daylight, they are basically nocturnal birds and therefore their eyesight is not so keen in strong light, I moved sideways and raised one arm. As his head turned to follow the movement, I grabbed with my other hand and, in spite of his protests, got a firm hold on him. He was placed carefully in a basket and was brought back to the hospital. We kept him over-night to make quite sure he was none the worse for his adventure.

Late the next evening, he was taken back to the Coombe and released. As the lid of the basket was raised, he hopped up on the edge, gripping with talons, shook himself so that his feathers settled sleekly to his body and then spread out his wings to fly silently up into the elm tree on the far side of the stream.

Another emergency phone call came late one afternoon soon after from an isolated farm on the moors a few miles from the coast. The farmer's wife explained that her husband was ill and her small son had just run into the house crying; he had been chased by a 'great big bird'. She went to look and when she saw it she quickly slammed the door shut. Could we help, as she must soon get out to the milking!

The farm was finally located after several wrong turnings and there, sure enough, was a *huge* gannet *and* he was very angry. There followed a scene which would have delighted lovers of slap-stick, as armed with only a towel I went into my matador act! This was no sick bird and he attacked straight away. After several flying tackles that landed me in oozy mud, I got the towel over his head and long neck, ignoring wings and large webbed feet thrashing furiously about, and managed to deposit him in the back of the van. Then back to the hospital, where we kept him several days to make sure he was fit. He never did recover his temper and I dare not think what those comments would have been if expressed in words. Bad tempered and flustered to the last, he was conveyed early one morning to a wild bit of cliff and suddenly, as the box opened, he saw the sea ahead of him. Several awkward steps took him to the cliff's edge where he shook himself, uttered one last rude word, spread his great wings and was away towards the horizon.

We began to think gannets were developing an affinity to farm life when yet another of them appeared on a peaceful rural scene to create mayhem.

One night in late spring, Olga received a phone call from a farmer near St Just. He told her that the police had advised him to ring the hospital after he had explained to them what he had found when he had gone to investigate a report that something was disturbing his herd of cows, grazing in a distant field. When he arrived there he had seen a large bird, its feet entangled in shreds of net, squawking and making short runs at the cows who, in turn, were bellowing and running all over the place. He captured the bird and shut it in an old car in his stable yard then rang for help. Olga told him I would pick up his 'queer bird' and bring it to the hospital with me when I came on duty.

He was waiting for me when I called about ten o'clock at night, and I arranged to pick up the bird early the next morning. The farmer told me he had managed to remove the strands of net from the bird's feet but it still had some on its beak.

When I arrived I crawled into the car and after some trouble removed the very irate gannet, the farmer assuring me he had never seen one of 'they' before.

Olga and I had a very difficult time at the hospital removing the net from his poor beak. He had a tangle the size of a table tennis ball wrapped around it, so tight that scissors were of little use. And he was quite a handful, being very fit, unlike so many birds that reach us ill and weak.

At last he was free and we could only assume that he must have dived for fish and gone through a trawl net, then fought his way free and headed inland to end up in the cow's field by an act of providence. We fed him up and kept him for several days to make sure he suffered no ill effects and then one morning he was released from the cliffs. His blue eyes glared with puzzlement and rage until they saw the sea. Then off he went like a bullet, joining up with several gannets who were flying off shore. I watched them all until they were too distant to be seen, with a feeling of thankfulness that he was back in his own element once more.

By now it will be apparent that gannets are something of a law unto themselves. But perhaps they should be allowed a few eccentricities. They are the largest and probably most spectacular of all our sea birds. Even the young ones in their steel-grey plumage speckled with white, have an imposing appearance, although it is not until their third year that they attain the snowy plumage of adulthood. At breeding time the colour of their heads deepens to a yellow-cream and the duck egg blue 'veins' on their thick legs and the long toes of their huge webbed feet also become more vivid. But the pointed flight feathers remain forever black as a reminder of their dark youth.

Many years ago, Mount's Bay was the scene of an incredible invasion of hundreds of gannets who were dive-bombing a huge shoal of fish. The sea boiled with spray as the great white birds plummeted through the glassy blue waves, folding their six-foot wing span just before the moment of entry. The fish were so plentiful that their pursuers did not bother to ascend to the traditional spectacular height to dive and spear their prey but merely rose a few feet above the water to plunge again. Finally the shoal turned and moved out to sea towards The Lizard and the gannets followed, many still diving but even more so sated with fish that they could only swim along behind, like an armada of white ships.

It is said that, over the years, a gannet may gradually become blinded by the continual impact of stinging water as it dives for food from great heights. For a while we wondered if this might have been the answer to the most puzzling gannet we have ever looked after.

This adult bird was brought to us one evening having been found wandering along the main road between Hayle and Camborne where it was rescued by an RAC patrol man. Aptly, he came in on 1st April and for the next twenty days had us all well and truly fooled.

When the patrol man arrived at the hospital he carried the gannet up the steps, cradled in his arms. The bird's head was quite free and he was making no attempt to struggle. This, in itself, was a puzzle. Of all the species we care for, the gannet is treated with utmost respect. Not only is he extremely powerful but a peck from his huge bill can slash flesh like a knife. There was something very wrong with a gannet who allowed itself to be handled so easily. Once set down on the office floor he promptly tucked his head under his wing and went to sleep. He was still sleeping when he was put in a cage in the annexe under infra-red heat.

For the next week our new patient remained there, his massive body an incongruous sight compared with his neighbours, the garden birds and jackdaws who were at that time undergoing similar 'intensive care' in their separate cages. The gannet did

Dodo, barn owl waiting for a phone call.

Bumble and Bee, two baby tawny owls reared here and later released successfully.

Baby tawny owl, Misty, reared up here and later released where it was found.

nothing except sleep, remaining motionless save for the times when he was shaken by spasms of shivering. He barely roused from his coma to swallow the mackerel that we hand-fed him, but the fish did stay down, so at least we knew he was receiving nourishment.

The 'April Fool' was certainly no trouble to look after but, because he reacted so passively to both the staff and his surroundings, we remembered the theory about gannet-blindness and began to fear that this might be what was wrong with the magnificent bird. However, when he did manage to open his eyes, we saw they were the normal glacial, gannet-blue and there was no sign of injury, no white spots of cataracts, nor the tell-tale clouded film that so often accompanies blindness.

At the end of his first week, our Fool was put in the annexe to the Guillemot House, with several guillemots next door for company. To begin with he seemed totally oblivious to the change in his surroundings, although he was spending more time awake. One morning he suddenly walked from his house into the outside pen. It was the first deliberate movement he had ever made. From then on he showed ever-increasing signs that he was returning from his trance-world to normality.

Fool's behaviour continued to fascinate us and we were thrilled because it seemed each day he was re-discovering life. He remained extraordinarily gentle but *everything* had to be touched and examined. Our wellingtons, his fish, the edge of the pond, even the guillemot's legs and feet all experienced the probing tap of his beak. His actions were always slow and thoughtful, as if the regained knowledge was being stored for future reference. At last we had conclusive evidence we had been hoping for, that his eyesight was unimpaired, when he began to take and eat, without any assistance, the mackerel we held out to him.

Our Fool went from strength to strength and, although gentle and courteous as ever, he began to walk restlessly up and down the front of his run, showing us quite plainly that he was longing to be

In Answer to the Cry

free. He was taken to our 'gannet launching pad' near Pendeen lighthouse on the north coast and, enigmatic to the end, took to the air without a moment's hesitation and flew out and away over the water, leaving us still totally mystified as to his illness.

XVI
Ducks and Other Patients

One of the most inspiring things, Pog and I have always felt, is to see a bird released again – perfect after injury or helplessness, into its own free life of the wild. Unhappily not all are fit to be given their freedom as one would wish. However some can happily accept their limitations, and do so with such pluck, that as long as they remain content, to deprive them of life has always seemed to us a betrayal of their will to survive.

Ducks especially are some of the many birds who have settled down to life in the sanctuary very happily, and they seem to have a rather steadying influence on the others around them. One December a female mallard duck was admitted, in very poor condition and with a badly injured left leg. The break had already set firmly in an awkward position. The foot was turned, and the leg stuck out almost at a right angle to the body. Pam tells from the records, how the hospital dealt with the situation, and of some others that followed.

There was nothing we could do for the leg but Miss Mallard had adjusted to her disability and was able to get around in a rather ungraceful dot and carry fashion. It soon became clear though that in the wild state she would quickly become the victim of a predator, of a fox perhaps, and so Mally stayed with us.

She settled in so well at the hospital that soon we had to change her name from 'Miss' to 'Mrs' when she started to lay eggs. She became a veritable one-duck egg factory, sitting on a clutch until she got bored with it, tossing the eggs out and then almost immediately producing a new batch.

As the months passed she played hostess to a succession of temporary patients in the run with its large pond which was now her home.

More than a year was to pass before Mrs Mallard's mother instincts could be shared with a mate. A young uninjured drake was brought to us who gloried under the splendid breed name of Blue Appleyard, apparently some sort of cross between ducks of different species. We called him 'Peter' and Mrs Mallard thought he was wonderful. Equally Peter fell passionately in love with the little lame duck.

They settled down to a life of happy domesticity and soon Mally was sitting tight on a clutch of seven eggs. Peter was a devoted husband and kept guard outside the little house where his 'missus' had her nest.

The hatching of the eggs was eagerly awaited but the date the ducklings were due to make their appearance came and passed. In the end even the patient Mrs Mallard gave up and we found the eggs floating on the pond. They were all addled with no sign of a duckling in any of them. Mrs Mallard and Peter remained unblessed by the patter of little webbed feet through all the time they were together.

Sadly, as time went on, Mrs Mallard's condition began to deteriorate. Through the summer she stayed fit and well, but the colder winter months began to take their toll. We brought her indoors and for a while she improved, but unfortunately then she lost strength and died.

Peter was later taken to a bird lover we know, who had given a home to several ducks in the past and he settled there quite happily with others of his kind.

One of the more unusual patients that Mrs Mallard had shared her run with was Mrs Feathers, a very large and rather fluttering

Ducks and Other Patients

Chinese goose, who had been brought from Gorran School, on the South Cornish coast near St Austell, where she had been one of their pets. The teacher and pupils who came with her were very concerned about her health and it was decided to leave her in our care for a while.

The goose was limping badly and, more mysterious, she was prone to fainting fits. The vet diagnosed a nervous condition which was causing her to pass out when she came under stress. She was given an injection and a few days later she was much improved in spirits though still rather shaky on her legs.

Some weeks after her arrival she was moved from her 'retreat' in a quiet run of her own, to a more spacious one with a big pond. There under the matronly influence of Mrs Mallard she was inspired to lay a beautiful large egg. She did not go to the trouble of making her own nest but deposited the egg with Mally's clutch and left it in her care. No objections were raised.

Mrs Feathers continued to thrive and at last we were able to tell Gorran School they could come and collect her. She left us on May Day fit and well.

Three weeks later Mrs Feathers was being carried up the hospital steps again in a state of total collapse, in a worse condition than on her first admittance. However we did learn something this time as to her domestic situation, and decided that here lay the source of her hysteria. She was part of a menage of four, sharing the affections of a gander with two other geese. We were not sure if she suffered from the 'vapours' out of jealousy of the other wives, or whether it was the over-amorous advance of her mate which upset her.

However she soon regained her strength and composure, and left us once more, at the beginning of June, a well-adjusted goose. This time the cure was permanent and we never had to treat her again. Apparently she had come to terms with her domestic problems.

Even more of a mystery than Mrs Feathers, were the two baby

shelducks brought to us one June, after they had been found abandoned on the sand dunes near Hayle. The ducklings soon settled down and by day they enjoyed the freedom of a pen on Green Hedges' lawn and by night they were put to bed in the hospital building.

A duckling's rate of growth is so rapid in the first few weeks of life it almost seems to get bigger before one's eyes. Within a week we began to notice a very curious phenomenon. One duckling was developing quite normally but the other remained almost as small as the day it had arrived. Hence, they became known as David and Goliath. Whilst Goliath grew enough for both of them, his little brother remained, so to speak, stranded in childhood. The only visible sign of illness was a skin disorder which left him with bare patches at his throat and neck. We supplemented David's diet with a mash of egg, milk, etc; but it was only after six long weeks that his 'growth switch' went on and he began the struggle to catch up with Goliath, who was by this time nearly full grown.

As David grew, feathers began to show through the duckling down he had retained all this time. But the strain of the sudden spurt in his development brought on an attack of rickets. Fortunately, a calcium additive in his feed checked the disease before he suffered permanent deformity. After all these trials and tribulations, he at last attained the same size as Goliath and soon the two were almost indistinguishable.

When they had moulted into their handsome plumage of bottle green, bold white, chestnut and black, they were released in the sheltered marshes near Marazion which act as a small sanctuary for water fowl.

In the summer, whilst our ducks are down a-dabbling, as Kenneth Grahame might say, high in the blue above, swifts whirl and call – well, not always. Sometimes these small masters of the air come to earth with a crunch. When they are brought to us, the usual explanation of their rescue is, 'I found it on the ground and it can't fly'.

Ducks and Other Patients

The neat, deep brown bird is handed over and examined to see if this is going to be merely another 'brief encounter' or a longer stay. The long scythe-shaped wings are carefully spread and searched for tell-tale swellings or the movement of broken bones. If the wings are undamaged, we turn our attention to the short, powerful legs and feet, whose pincer grip with needle-sharp claws is more animal than bird-like. If here, too, all is normal, the swift's feathers behind the head and on and under the wings are gently parted. These are the favourite hiding place of unwelcome 'passengers'. Swifts are prone to collecting a strange, spiderish tick that we seldom see on other birds. They can be as big as the end of a little finger and when disturbed scuttle through the feathers with stomach-turning speed. They are the most foul of parasites and we have seen many swifts die because their strength has been literally sucked away by these 'stowaways'. If found, we remove them with tweezers but, with luck, our swift is tick free and it is given its last test and held out on the palm of the hand.

For a few seconds the bird lies there warm and still, except for the beating of its heart. Then, from inside the frail body, grows a vibration of unbelievable power. The wings might start to flutter but nothing matches the speed of this hidden dynamo that unfailingly tells us all is well with the swift.

The reason it has been brought to us is that once a swift lands on the ground it cannot rise into the air again without assistance. The spread of its wings is great in comparison with the length of its body and its short legs are so adapted to clinging on to walls, or other steep nesting sites, that even an uninjured swift can only crawl helplessly across the ground.

Our 'brief encounter' swift is rested for an hour or so and then taken up to the meadows behind the hospital. Here, we toss it gently in the air. The wings open to catch the wind and with rapid beats lift the swift higher and higher as it swoops and circles in joyous freedom.

Sometimes though, these birds arrive injured and, despite

In Answer to the Cry

trying to match their diet of insects caught on the wing, we face great problems in feeding them. A big headache too can be a baby swift that has fallen from its nest and is not yet old enough to take its place in the world. A few years ago one such youngster arrived at the hospital but, from the start, he had a voracious appetite. He quickly learnt to take the flies, chopped mealworms and tiny shreds of raw meat and, in his eagerness for more would even try to gulp down our finger ends. He was called Mighty Mouth out of respect for his swallowing capabilities. A few days later he was joined by Minnie Mouth. Minnie was of a more reticent nature and we had to be very careful to keep Mighty at bay whilst she was fed. For his indiscriminate habit of engulfing anything connected with food in his elastic jaws included Minnie's head!

Mighty and Minnie thrived and in a fortnight they were considered ready for release. As luck would have it, we were brought an adult 'brief encounter' swift and, hoping it would give the youngsters a lead, all three were taken up to the meadows. After a countdown of 'Three Two One' the swifts were launched into the air and they flew away together.

Such a happy ending was not anticipated for one swift brought to us within the last year. A young couple found the bird on the roadside and at first it was thought it had somehow become entangled in very fine nylon thread. But when Olga and Peggy started to unwind this, they found to their horror that the thread had been deliberately *sewn* through the skin of the wings and throat, binding them together.

The thread was snipped and and gently drawn back through the skin and the swift was freed from its hideous enchainment. By some miracle no vital parts had been damaged and it was put in a warm hospital cage to recover from shock. In an hour it was frantically crawling up the front of the cage and when it was taken out its 'all is well' dynamo whirred into life. It was taken out into open ground to try its wings and immediately soared into the air and away.

Ducks and Other Patients

It is almost impossible to comprehend the mentality of such torturers and, fortunately, incidences of premeditated cruelty are far outweighed by acts of heartfelt concern. So often people will go to the lengths of physical discomfort, not to mention hazard, in their spontaneous response to the plight of a helpless bird.

As an example of this, one mid-June, summer had disappeared to be replaced by an almost wintry squall. The wind got up and drove the sea into high, choppy waves, rain pelted against the window pane. When halfway through a late duty, Neil's bell rang to proclaim the arrival of a new patient. A lady and a young girl appeared at the office door. The lady was carrying a rolled towel and poking out of the centre was an enormous black beak. She explained that they were visitors to the district and, whilst she and her daughter had been walking over the Mousehole rocks, they had seen a very large black bird blown down into the waves a little way from the shore. They had waded out into the sea to waist depth and managed somehow to rescue the bird from a watery grave. Both were soaked to the skin and, after handing over the towel and its contents, were anxious to get into dry clothes and went off down the steps without more ado.

The beak was unrolled from the towel and behind it was revealed a mass of soggy, black feathers and trembling pink flesh. It was immediately apparent from the bird's huge size, that this was neither rook nor crow but their mighty relative the raven.

Ravens usually breed in solitary pairs and because this one had been found at Mousehole it seemed certain to be one of the couple who, for several years, had ruled a small pine wood on the coastal footpath between this village and Lamorna Cove. They often flew over Mousehole and down on to the rocks, distinguished by their gutteral croaking and the silhouette of their wedge-shaped tail and broad 'fingered' wings. But the real place to watch them was on a windy day near their nesting site, when they enchanted the eye with aerobatic displays, swooping, somersaulting and gliding with high-spirited skill. Their *pièce de résistance* was to fly on their

In Answer to the Cry

backs a little way before flicking out in a victory roll.

'How are the mighty fallen' was the message that seemed to come from the bedraggled object on the office floor. Because the raven had been rescued from the sea, providence was tempted and he was promptly named Jonah.

Jonah's eyes were glazed with shock and he was trembling so violently that a few drops of 'Rescue Remedy' were given to revive him. This liquid essence of wild flowers and other ingredients had beeen recommended as having positively elixir-like qualities. It had been used with variable success on birds suffering from shock but Jonah certainly seemed to enjoy it.

Next he was put in front of a fan heater to dry off and gradually his feathers began to fluff out and hide the pink skin of his bony shoulders and drum-stick thighs. His rocking legs become more rock-like and his frightened eyes took on more than a vestige of intelligence. In fact, when perfectly dry, Jonah was a majestic bird. Two feet long from beak tip to the point of his wedged tail, he had a bristly moustache, shaggy throat feathers and a heavy 'mantle'. When he moved his plumage sheened from black to purple-blue. He was put in a basket by the fire overnight, with a note left on top warning 'Beware of the Beak'!

In the morning we found Jonah standing on the lid of his basket and fully recovered from his traumatic experience of the previous day. He regarded us benignly and showed no sign of panic at his strange surroundings. Outside, summer had returned and the sun was shining strongly in a real Cornish-blue sky. Jonah was carried to the top of the steps beyond the gull runs where he took off from outstretched hands to beat a lazy and unerring course along the coast towards Lamorna.

He still flies over the hospital with his mate, and every year they are joined in training flights by three or four youngsters. No doubt Jonah includes in his instructions dire warnings about the perils of flying too close to the sea.

This last episode is typical of the selfless behaviour of the many

Ducks and Other Patients

hundreds of people who have brought birds to us here. The trouble and risks they are willing to take when they find them injured or in need, brings home to one how widespread is the love and concern for our birds. Perhaps it is partly because the wild bird, with its freedom of the land air and sea, seems somehow to give us release from the cares of this world and to unite us in that freedom.

Those of us who have worked for these lovely creatures and have been allowed to make a close individual contact with them, feel we have been more than fully rewarded by the privilege of their trust. We also feel we should be failing them if this hospital does not remain open to receive them when they need us most.

XVII
Survival

Pog and I always tried to take each day as it came, conserving all our energies to solve a problem when actually faced with it. But perhaps at the back of our minds has been the thought, 'What of the future?' Survival is the vital word, not only for the sanctuary but for each bird that comes for help. The sanctity of life itself is realised as the prospect of near death changes to a gleam of hope, followed by life restored to its full beauty and fulfilment.

A bird responds in an amazing way to the helping hand that sustains it with love and understanding. Once this confidence is won, half the battle is over. A link is established between the bird and those looking after it, which can last even beyond recovery and release.

We had many instances in the old days as to how birds we had cared for must have spread the news to their wild friends, so that we could be called to the rescue when needed.

If we heard the warning cry of a jackdaw or herring gull we instantly set out to find where it came from. We would find an injured bird on the ground, a baby fallen from a nest, or a cat on the prowl, with the agitated adult birds circling round uttering their frantic calls. Then, as we picked up the injured bird, or sent off the cat, *at once* the warnings would cease, the birds overhead would fly off, showing quite plainly that now all was well again.

Another evidence of their trust is a moving one, shown by jackdaws in particular. We have found that this highly intelligent

Survival

bird is gifted with an amazing memory, which enables him to distinguish one human being from another, and also to remember the place he can go to if in dire need of help.

Several times we have had the sad experience of finding one of our daily visitors to our ever open birds' balcony, at our cottage, sitting inside hunched up in a corner or on a bough looking only half aware of what is going on. We wait until dusk, quietly close the window, and then take him into our hands and put him into a basket prepared with a warm blanket, food and water. He makes no resistance on being caught and we get the feeling that this is what he was hoping for. He may not die until the morning but usually passes away in his sleep during the night.

Rooks and crows also appreciate human friendship if once established. Like jackdaws, their wings would flick and feathers rose in pleasure when they were greeted by Pog at her studio window. It was here that one of our saddest experiences will always be remembered. I told of this in *The Cry of a Bird* but think I must record it once more.

Nigger, a jackdaw reared up by Pog in her studio, never lost contact with her after release, but flew into her room every morning to have breakfast with her, on her bed. This strangely happy and complete friendship lasted for ten years. Then one morning, instead of his landing on the window sill as usual, there was a flutter of wings as he tried to get to the sill but fell instead to the ground below. Pog ran out to find him lying with *both* legs bleeding and broken. He must have met with a terrible accident, and how it happened we shall never know. He just had strength enough to get to the window and safety. This confidence in us touched us deeply and made hard the sad decision we had to take. We knew that Nigger, who belonged to the wild and free, must never be allowed to realise what had happened.

As Pog held him in her arms, fear seemed to leave him and he slept. Lying peacefully then in her hands, Nigger was helped to go into that deeper sleep from which there is no return. Though we had to sever the link of this bird's mortal life, he himself, by his supreme and unfailing faith in us, had woven a thread of gold which will never be broken.

Having lived closely with wild birds for so many years as we have done, we have learnt a very great deal from them. Their faithfulness to their mates, their devotion to their offspring and their courage in adversity are lessons from which we can all learn.

They have also shown us how different species vary in character. The seagulls, always independent, accept us but never wish to get intimate, keeping us firmly in our place. Gannets never even contemplate a contact with humans. As Pog always said, with their big cold blue eyes they seem to belong to the ice age, remote and distant.

The little diving birds, the guillemots, razorbills and puffins who are brought here, once adapted to their new surroundings, accept us as part of the landscape. Their real home is the deep ocean and the wild rocky shore where they have their young on sheltered ledges or in burrows.

The gulls make use of human habitations by commandeering the roofs and chimneys for their nests, but once the young are reared they take command of the sky, swooping down and flying high, uttering those calls which keep one in constant touch with wild life. Many nest and roost on St Clement's Island just off shore and when disturbed by visitors they rise in a huge flock uttering war-like cries, warning the invaders it is no place for them.

Not only have we met many types of birds over these long years, we have also learnt much of our fellow human beings; some so sensitive that they do not have to be told what our hospital stands for; others so uncomprehending that they just cannot understand what it is all about. A few have said, 'It's all right, but you know, it's only a drop in the ocean'; to which we reply, 'Yes, but the ocean is made of drops'.

We have asked ourselves sometimes, when tired and weary, 'Has it all been worth while?' The answer has always been, 'Yes',

Survival

when we thought of all the thousands of birds who have found peace and security with us, some to recover completely, others to die; but even so, something has been gained, a quiet end instead of slow starvation or suffering.

From Jacko, our first bird in 1928, until November of 1977 a total of 27,780 birds have been brought to our hospital. Pog and I were responsible up to 1959 for 4,066 we received, and the remaining 23,714 were handled by the staff appointed in 1960. They, like us, feel it has been, and always will be, right to fight for the survival of our sanctuary, and are determined to do so.

Our releases each year have consistently been about 34 per cent, some years a little higher when fewer oiled birds have been admitted.

It must be remembered that wild birds only allow themselves to be caught when their condition is desperate. Therefore the number of complete recoveries is bound to be relatively small and the number of deaths great. But the helping hands are always here doing their utmost to care for them all.

Time passes and we must turn our thoughts again to the question of how the future *can* be made secure. We know the roots of our sanctuary are strong after these fifty years of growth; now comes the necessity of facing up to our present crisis to maintain its permanent life. This can only be done by the continued generosity of all those who realise the debt we owe to the birds for contributing to the beauty and happiness of our lives by their very existence. To come to their rescue in sickness and suffering is the way we can best repay the debt.

Only lately this feeling has been shown in the wonderful response we had to a sympathetic article in the magazine *Woman*, written by one who had real understanding of our needs. Her message got across in such a genuine way that once more the letters came with gifts both large and small, encouraging us to carry on. We could hardly believe the amount we received, just over £1,000. And this was crowned with another £1,000 from HRH

In Answer to the Cry

the Aga Khan as a result of the article. He wrote how pleased he had been to read it and wishing us well in our efforts to carry on. How grateful we were to him, as we are to those other bird lovers who stand so staunchly by us, making it possible for us to exist from year to year until our aim is achieved and permanency assured.

More generous letters came from far away Australia following yet another kind journalist's article. Some of her readers wrote wanting to hear more about our sanctuary and anxious to help.

Children once more were full of concern for our birds. A teacher of English in Wolverhampton had visited the hospital after having read *The Cry of a Bird* with her class at school. She showed the greatest interest, and on her return from her holiday she was able to give the children a first-hand account of what she had seen. She also gave each one a copy of the article in *Woman*. The children's imagination was aroused and we received thirty-three letters expressing their pleasure with fervent hopes for our future.

Only a short time ago a small boy, on holiday in Mousehole, came to the hospital door and nervously asked how much he must pay to go round. At being told 'nothing' he looked astonished and then wandered round on his own looking intently at the different birds. When one of the girls told him how all the birds would have died had they not been brought to them to be treated and looked after, he showed real pleasure in a quiet way. A few days later, when it was almost dark and Pam was locking up for the night, the office door opened, a small hand thrust a piece of paper into hers and a voice said shyly, 'That's for you'; and the boy ran quickly away down the steps. On the piece of paper he had drawn an owl with 'Thank you - very Kind' coming out of its mouth. Beside the owl was Neil's bell. Then he wrote his own message:

> I hope you will look at this because
> it is what I think of you:
> Very kind
> I hope all the birds get well.

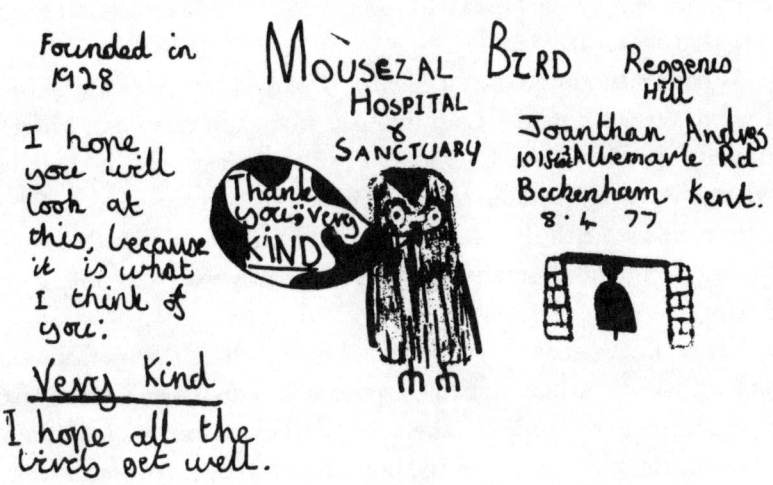

Jonathan's Letter

An experience Pog and I never forgot happened in the days when we were working on our own. After all the morning work at the hospital was done we used to lock all the doors, and go down to Green Hedges for a quick mid-day meal. One day on our return, to our dismay we found the outside collection box was missing. We looked up and down the hill but no one was in sight. We knew the box was heavy with money and felt very worried. We told our Mousehole policeman who said he would do what he could.

About two days later I was at Green Hedges, preparing our meal, when from the window I saw Pog coming down the path, carrying the money box and followed by two young boys. They all came in. Pog handed me the box, standing behind the boys, and said, 'These boys came a few minutes ago and told me they had found a money box in the fields above the hospital and felt sure it belonged to the birds.' Pog had then said, 'Will you show me where it is?' They all climbed up the steep wall into the field, and there, half hidden under the hedge, was the box. I saw Pog looking

In Answer to the Cry

at me (unseen by the boys) with eyebrows raised in query and with a big smile on her face.

What a situation to be faced with! I played for time and asking the boys to sit down, I examined the box with care. 'No hinges broken. The lock intact. Oh, look! in the slit on top of the box where the money is put in there is a *pound note*, only just inside. The person who stole the box could *easily* have pulled it out with a pin.' I paused and looked at the boys, both intently watching me in an anxious way.

Then I knew what to say: 'Do you know, I think that person was suddenly sorry he had robbed the poor sick birds, so he left the box in the hedge and ran away. Then you two boys came. It's just like a miracle, the way you found the box.' I looked up, their faces were transfigured; one leant forward with a happy smile and said, 'So *now* you believe in miracles!!'

Pog in the meantime was almost choking with suppressed laughter, I feeling slightly guilty about the 'whiteness' of the miracle, as the boys ran off on top of the world.

Another memory comes to mind. One day I was going down the hill when I was met by a very small boy holding something closely in his tiny hands. He came up to me and said with a distressed look on his face, 'She never ought to have done it. She said I could keep it and now she says I've got to get rid of it. I found it as a little baby and made it a home in my cupboard. It's grown and it's all right. You *do* take in mice at the hospital, don't you?'

Speechless, again I played for time and at last I said, 'Well, let's bring it up there, and see what can be done.'

When we reached the safety of the bird room, I took the little thing out of his hands. To my relief it was a minute field mouse and looked perfectly fit. I gave the boy some bits of cheese and biscuit so that his mouse would have something to eat, and told him we would go up to the fields and find a place to let it go, where it would be safe but free to lead its own life and find some friends. All went well and the child was cheerful again.

Survival

Then there was the little boy who came up one day holding a jackdaw with an injured wing. When I held out my hands to take it, the boy drew back, looking very miserable, and said, 'You do grow new wings here, don't you?'

'We do our very best, and anyway your bird will be safe and well looked after,' I said. His expression changed to a happy smile and he gave me the bird.

Although our work is first for the birds we feel strongly that it means something very important for the children. In answer to those grown-ups who sometimes say it is wrong to spend money on birds when one thinks of the starving children and the sufferings of others in distant parts of the world, our reply has always been to say that if an awareness of suffering can be awakened in a child, and he is given the opportunity of *doing* something about it, this compassion will last all through life and will develop into an awareness of *all* suffering; and isn't that the only hope for the world?

The sanctuary *must* survive. The children need it as much as the birds.

Eleven years have now passed since the wreck of the *Torrey Canyon*. Now as I come to the end of my book the cries of the oiled birds can be heard yet again. The giant tanker *Amoco Cadiz* has this week run on to the rocks off Brittany spilling out twice as much oil as did the *Torrey Canyon* and bringing a new black cloud of suffering and death to the wild life of the sea.

What can be done? How can atonement be made?

The answer must be the concern of all and everyone of us.

Epilogue

It is difficult to say when the slowing up really began for Pog. All her life she had been so full of activities both of mind and body. I always said she had missed her vocation by not being wrecked on a desert island; her ingenuity in making something out of nothing was amazing. When we left Green Hedges there was no room anywhere for our grandmother's wardrobe which had been with us all our lives. It must have been well over a hundred years old, still in perfect condition. I did not know *what* to do with it. Pog said, 'I'll deal with that,' and proceeded to take it to pieces and make a garden shed out of it, with sunny sliding windows, shelves and fitments, and the door of course one of those from the wardrobe. The floor she made from an iron-framed wire mattress on which bits of wood from the wardrobe were fixed. In this she raised tomatoes and seedlings of every sort. Friends called it her solarium.

Her most treasured possession was her studio. Reading and music meant a great deal to her, as was shown by her collection of books and gramophone records. Chaliapin as Boris, and Toscanini records were the most precious. The last time she ever went back to London was to hear Toscanini conducting at the old Queen's Hall, just before the Second World War.

Her heart was in her wood carving, her great happiness in her wild birds, always her constant companions. Her imagination ranged over many fields. With her very original sense of fun she would write most humorous rhymes — sheets with illustrations of herself and our sister Mary dancing through Mousehole's winding streets to visit their friends.

Many a happy evening was spent in the studio with our friends when Pog manipulated her own puppets in a little wooden theatre she had made. She wrote the dramatic script for them herself, shown with suitable background music on the gramophone.

Other nights there would be discussions and arguments over every subject under the sun, lasting till after midnight when her brain would become the most brilliant. Those were happy days.

Poor Pog felt a terrible sense of frustration as her daily tasks became more and more difficult through failing health and eyesight. 'The clock running down' was how our understanding doctor described it. But her indomitable spirit kept her going until just two weeks before the end. Then she accepted the fact that she could not now leave her bed. As her strength slowly and quietly diminished, she mercifully suffered no pain and slept most of the time. But her face would light up with the old happiness when Tapper the rook came in at the window for his bits of special food, keeping her in daily touch with her beloved birds.

One afternoon I was sitting near her when I noticed a change in her breathing as she slept. Then — two little sighs — and silence. I have never seen, or heard of, a more beautiful farewell to life.

I have no fear of death. I feel it is the most exciting moment in life, to find out what happens next. Pog has crossed over and is now at her new beginning.

I slept in the studio that night, as I had been doing for several weeks. I shall never forget the utter calm and peace that prevailed, with her wooden sculpture 'The Spirit of Flame' raising his hands in benediction, and her 'Man Above', guarding us, with his vision of something beyond.

In the morning I woke early and stood beside her. Her face had the loveliness of a happy child, all the lines of frustration smoothed away, her life here fulfilled, and over.

Her ashes lie amongst the roses beneath her studio window, resting beside Neverest, the jackdaw who shared so much of his happy life with her. Our little Peardrop who finally folded his wings only ten days later also lies beside her, with a cloud of blue forget-me-nots over them all.

APPENDIX

*Species of Wild and Domestic Birds
admitted to the Hospital since 1960*

In Answer to the Cry
SPECIES OF WILD BIRDS
ADMITTED TO THE HOSPITAL SINCE 1960

Auk, Little
Bittern
Blackbird
Blackcap
Brambling
Bullfinch
Bunting, Corn
– Reed
Buzzard, Common
– Honey
Chaffinch
Chiffchaff
Coot
Cormorant
Corncrake
Crane, Demoiselle
Crow
Cuckoo
Curlew
Diver, Great Northern
– Black Throated
– Red Throated
Dove, Collared
– Turtle
Duck, Eider
– Mandarin
– Shoveler
– Tufted
Dunlin
Egret, Little
Fieldfare

Flycatcher, Pied
– Spotted
Gannet
Godwit, Bar-Tailed
– Black-Tailed
Goldcrest
Goldfinch
Goose, Canada
– Greylag
– White-Fronted
Grebe, Little
– Slavovian
Greenfinch
Guillemot
Gull, Black Headed
– Common
– Greater Black Backed
– Herring
– Lesser Black Backed
– Little
Hawfinch
Heron
Hoopoo
Jackdaw
Jay
Kestrel
Kingfisher
Kittiwake
Knot
Lapwing
Linnet

Magpie
Mallard
Martin, House
— Sand
Merganser, Red Breasted
Merlin
Moorhen
Nightjar
Nuthatch
Owl, Barn
— Little
— Long Eared
— Tawny
— Short Eared
Oyster Catcher
Partridge
Petrel, Fulmar
— Storm
Phalarope, Grey
Pheasant
Pigeon, Feral
— Wood
Pipit, Meadow
— Rock
— Tree
Plover, Golden
— Grey
— Ringed
Pochard
Puffin
Quail
Raven
Razorbill
Redwing

Robin
Rook
Sanderling
Sandpiper
Scoter, Common
— Velvet
Shag
Shearwater, Cory's
— Manx
Shelduck
Shorelark
Siskin
Skylark
Skua, Great
Snipe
Sparrow, Hedge
— House
Sparrowhawk
Starling
Stint
Swallow
Swan, Bewick's
— Mute
— Whooper
Swift
Teal
Tern, Arctic
— Common
— Little
Thrush, Mistle
— Song
Tit, Blue
— Coal
— Great

In Answer to the Cry

– Long Tailed
Tree Creeper
Turnstone
Twite
Wagtail, Grey
– Pied
– Yellow
Warbler, Reed
– Willow
– Wood

Water Rail
Wheatear
Whimbrel
Whinchat
Whitethroat
Wigeon
Woodpecker, Green
– Lesser Spotted
Wren
Yellowhammer

TOTAL: 150 species

SPECIES OF DOMESTIC BIRDS ADMITTED

Budgerigar
Canary
Cockatiel
Dove, White
– Barbary
Duck, Aylesbury
– Blue Appleyard
– Khaki Campbell
– Muscovy
Goose, Chinese
Lovebird, Peach-Faced

Mule (Aviary Finch)
Mynah
Parakeets, Ring Neck
Parrots, African Green
– African Grey
Peacock, Blue
– White
Pheasant, Chinese
– Silver
Poultry
Waxbill